CELTIC WISDOM

For Tom, with love.

LION

CELTIC WISDOM
Treasures from Ireland

Cindy Thomson

A Lion Book, an imprint of
Lion Hudson plc,
Wilkinson House, Jordan Hill Road, Oxford OX2 8DR, England
www.lionhudson.com
UK ISBN 978 0 7459 5325 0
US ISBN 978 0 8254 7842 0

First edition 2008
10 9 8 7 6 5 4 3 2 1 0

Text acknowledgments
pp. 6, 14, 41, 78, 81, 82, 85, 90: Scripture quotations taken from the *Holy Bible, New International Version*, copyright © 1973, 1978, 1984 International Bible Society. Used by permission of Zondervan and Hodder & Stoughton Limited. All rights reserved. The 'NIV' and 'New International Version' trademarks are registered in the United States Patent and Trademark Office by International Bible Society. Use of either trademark requires the permission of International Bible Society. UK trademark number 1448790.
pp. 77, 87: Extracts from the Authorized Version of the Bible (The King James Bible), the rights in which are vested in the Crown, are reproduced by permission of the Crown's Patentee, Cambridge University Press.
pp. 8, 44: Scripture quotations are taken from the *Holy Bible, New Living Translation*, copyright © 1996. Used by permission of Tyndale House Publishers, Inc., Wheaton, Illinois 60189. All rights reserved.
Author acknowledgments
I would like to thank Martin Farrell; Dr Tim Campbell, Director of the Saint Patrick Centre; and Karen Robbins, for their assistance and critique. Any errors are mine alone.

A catalogue record for this book is available from the British Library

Typeset in 10.5/13 Photina MT
Printed and bound in Singapore

Distributed by:
UK: Marston Book Services Ltd, PO Box 269, Abingdon, Oxon OX14 4YN
USA: Trafalgar Square Publishing, 814 N. Franklin Street, Chicago, IL 60610
USA Christian Market: Kregel Publications, PO Box 2607, Grand Rapids, MI 49501

CONTENTS

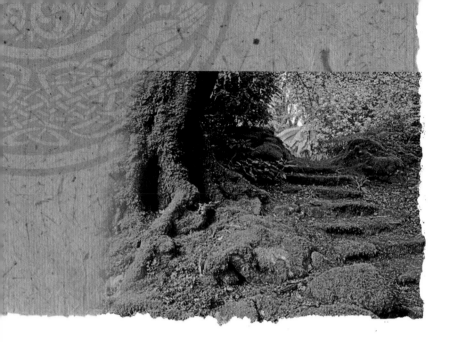

HOW THE
ANCIENT IRISH
FOUND THE
CHRISTIAN PATH

Stand at the crossroads and look;
ask for the ancient paths,
ask where the good way is, and walk in it,
and you will find rest for your souls.

JEREMIAH 6:16

The Path from Slave to Saint

In the north of Ireland in the fifth century a royal clan lacked slaves. A bevy of boisterous raiders, who were promised cattle and choice goods such as gold and fine cloth, stood ready to answer the call. This gang of marauders patrolled the coast and inland rivers of Britain near modern-day Wales. When the opportunity presented itself, they snatched unsuspecting folks who had come to the shore or along the riverbanks to dig for clams or wash clothes. Such raids were common on both sides of the Irish Sea, resulting in terror as families were torn apart. Ireland's famous patron saint, Patrick, first arrived in Ireland in such a manner. An unanticipated consequence of these slave raids, however, was the exchange of cultures and religions.

Christians lived in Ireland prior to Patrick's kidnapping, probably having come from Britain or continental Europe. Some natives, influenced by the cultural exchange, may have come to the religion because of it. However it happened, Christians did exist in Ireland at that time, for there would be no other reason Pope Celestine would have sent Palladius to Ireland as the island's first bishop in 431. His mission would have been to attend to a body of believers. St Prosper of Aquitaine, a contemporary, recorded this event. Palladius stayed in Ireland a short time, founding only three small churches.

Decades earlier Patrick escaped his captors after six long years of tending sheep and returned to his home. During his captivity he remembered his Christian upbringing and prayed constantly. In the years that followed, he devoted himself to God and to the church. One night he dreamed the Irish were calling to him and bidding him to return. He did return, shortly after Palladius left, according to most scholars. Patrick ministered not to the transplanted Christians, but to the native Irish. The fact that this had not been done earlier might explain why Christianity had not taken hold under Palladius and others. It was not until after

Patrick arrived for the second time as a missionary to the island that the fire of Christianity began to burn brightly.

Shining Light on the Path

The symbolism of the shamrock helps illustrate how Patrick related Christianity to the beliefs the pagan Irish already held. The native Irish had a particular reverence for triads – groups of three connected people or things. In fact, anything spoken of or explained in three ways signified its importance.

Legend says that Patrick used the ubiquitous shamrock to help explain the triune God: one plant, three leaves; one God, three persons. There is no evidence of this, and, because of their reverence for triads, the culture would have accepted the idea quite readily anyway. But the story does illustrate how willingly the native Irish accepted the Christian faith. Many aspects of Christianity were not big leaps for the pagan Irish. Just as they accepted the idea of the trinity, it was not difficult for them to move from worshipping creation and many gods to worshipping the Creator and the one true God.

Triads were recorded with the advent of written language in Ireland and can be found in some of its earliest records, such as the *Yellow Book of Lecan*, a medieval manuscript written sometime in the late fourteenth century. But undoubtedly they were handed down orally from even earlier times. Some examples:

Three candles that illumine every darkness: truth, nature, knowledge.

Three silences that are better than speech: silence during instruction, silence during music, silence during preaching.

Three excellences of dress: elegance, comfort, lastingness.

Three clouds that most obscure Wisdom's glance: forgetfulness, half-knowledge, ignorance.

The triad took on new importance in the light of Christianity. The blessing of three, Father, Son and Holy Spirit, was a natural fit. St Brendan, one of those who later followed Patrick's path, is said to have repeated this triad, taught to him by his foster mother Ita: there are three things beloved by God – true faith, simplicity and charity. And conversely, three things God despises – being cross, doing wrong and the love of money. There are many Irish triads that reflect Christian values, such as, 'There are three ways to love: with the heart, with the mind and with the soul.'

The faith spread slowly but steadily, gaining momentum in the sixth century with the age of monasticism; and as it grew and matured, it spawned some of Christianity's most respected and cherished individuals. How all this occurred in the span of just a few hundred years is perhaps one of history's mysteries. While some Christians held powerful positions, such as Columcille, a member of the powerful O'Neill clan, others were mere scribes and poor missionaries – a testament to how God used the ordinary to achieve the extraordinary.

History reveals that the Emerald Isle was a place where Christianity was able to escape annihilation during what has been called the Dark Ages, which lasted from the fifth to the eleventh century. The era in Ireland was referred to as the Golden Age of Christianity, a remarkable time that is romantically portrayed in the saying, 'Ireland: It's the one place on earth that heaven has kissed with melody and mirth, meadow and mist.'

Ireland, through her tradition of scholarship, her devotion to a form of Christianity that did not depend on Rome's leadership (Rome had fallen by that time), and her very location – a remote island thought to literally be at the end of the earth – was just the place to preserve the faith. There, beyond the reaches of Roman and barbaric invasions and in spite of the later Nordic terrors, a religion that was losing its hold in many parts of Europe found sanctuary. But the Irish people were not content to keep the faith ensconced in the stone cells of far-flung monasteries. They took what they had been blessed with and spread it throughout the island and to the European continent, not with the might of swords – as would occur later in Europe during the Crusades – not even with oratory or priest-led celebratory masses. While these things may have taken place in some form, there was a different focus in Ireland. The Irish Christians added their wisdom to the melody and mirth of the common people who longed to be closer to the Giver of Life.

The druidic system prevalent in ancient Ireland, known for its secretiveness, may have been losing favour by the time Christianity emerged. Christianity, by contrast, was open to all, and all were invited to learn its truths. Free from the invading warfare Europe was enduring, Ireland was uniquely positioned to nourish the new religion – just at the time that writing was emerging there. Utilizing the concept of an *anamcara* – what today would be called an accountability partner or a confessor – the early Irish Christians worked shoulder to shoulder with the common people and passed on their wisdom in stories and sayings.

Patrick and the early Celtic Christians spread their faith throughout Ireland. As the centuries forged onward, their legacy blessed many more people than Patrick could have ever imagined when he wrote:

... without regard to danger, I make known God's gift and the eternal comfort he provides; that I spread God's name everywhere dutifully and without fear so that after my death I may leave a legacy to so many thousands of people.

FROM ST PATRICK'S *CONFESSION*

PATRICK

I cannot keep silent, nor would it be proper, so many favours and graces has the Lord deigned to bestow on me in the land of my captivity. For after chastisement from God, and recognizing him, our way to repay him is to exalt him and confess his wonders before every nation under heaven.

FROM ST PATRICK'S CONFESSION

Patrick's Life

Patrick was born in the late fourth century. The exact dates he lived are unclear. We have two writings from St Patrick: his *Confession* and a letter titled 'The Letter to the Soldiers of Coroticus'. Other writings are attributed to him, but there is no assurance that he actually wrote them, and even some indication that they were written in a later period.

The *Confession* contains a brief biography beginning with Patrick's capture by the Irish. He states, 'I did not, indeed, know the true God; and I was taken into captivity in Ireland with many thousands of people, according to our deserts, for quite drawn away from God, we did not keep his precepts.'

So Patrick, who some believe was known as Maewyn Succat at that time, was taken away from his family of Christians and away from the influence of the Romanized church to a land of pagans. And yet, it was there, during his lonely years of shepherding for his slave master, that he found God and began to trust Him:

> And there the Lord opened my mind to an awareness of my unbelief...
> he watched over me before I knew him, and before I learned sense or even
> distinguished between good and evil, and he protected me, and consoled me as
> a father would his son.

Many times in the *Confession* Patrick relates his unwillingness to keep silent about the wonders of God. He makes a number of humble admissions. But most critical to our understanding of Patrick is the story of his spiritual life:

> But after I reached Hibernia [Latin for Ireland] I used to pasture the flock each
> day and I used to pray many times a day. More and more did the love of God,
> and my fear of him and faith increase, and my spirit was moved so that in a day
> [I said] from one up to a hundred prayers, and in the night a like number.

One night Patrick heard a voice telling him that he would soon depart for his native land on a ship that was waiting for him. He had to walk 200 miles to a place he had never been before. When he got there he found that the barbarians on board would not let him accompany them without his partaking in a pagan ritual, which he refused to do. He walked away, praying, but before he got very far he was called back. They had reconsidered and he was welcomed aboard.

The trip across the sea took only three days, but they travelled on land through an uninhabited area for nearly a month. During this time food ran out, and the captain asked Patrick to appeal to his God. Patrick replied, 'Be converted by faith with all your heart to my Lord God, because nothing is impossible for him...' Patrick foretold that food would soon appear, and then a herd of wild pigs ran into their path. The men killed and feasted, and were thus saved from starvation.

Eventually Patrick was reunited with his family in Britain. There are some unrecorded years during which it is speculated that he trained in monasteries in Gaul or perhaps in Britain. One night a man named Victoricus visited him in a dream, bearing many letters from Ireland. He gave one to Patrick that read 'The Voice of the Irish'. Immediately Patrick heard the voices of those he'd known in Ireland crying out together, 'We beg you, holy youth, that you shall come and shall walk again among us.' Later confirmation came in a dream when he heard words coming from 'within me or beside me', saying, 'He who gave his life for you, he it is who speaks within you.'

And so Patrick returned to his place of enslavement. While the number of conversions to the faith that Patrick's preaching evoked is extraordinary, what is equally admirable is the fact that he went voluntarily to where he had suffered at the hands of others and where his life had often been threatened.

It must have taken great courage and a keen sense of obedience to God for Patrick to put himself once again in harm's way:

> *... daily I expect to be murdered or betrayed or reduced to slavery if the occasion arises. But I fear nothing because of the promises of Heaven; for I have cast myself into the hand of Almighty God, who reigns everywhere...*

The mission was clear to the former slave: 'So are we seeing, and so it is fulfilled; behold, we are witnesses because the Gospel has been preached as far as the places beyond which no man lives.'

Patrick's mission to Ireland is significant because of the lasting effect it had. Finally, Patrick desired that his legacy would be passed on: 'I wish only that you, too, would make greater and better efforts. This will be my pride, for "a wise son makes a proud father"' (a reference to Proverbs 10:1 and 15:20).

There is something to be learned from writings of other ancient scribes. Generally attributed to a fifth-century bard named Fiacc, *The Hymn of Fiacc* – believed by most scholars to have actually been written in the seventh or eighth century – is an ancient text on the life of St Patrick. Since Patrick does not tell us in his own writings what he did from the time he returned to Britain after his enslavement to the time he went back to Ireland, we depend on this document and others after it, which contend that Patrick studied all over Europe. *The Hymn of Fiacc* describes the time of his return: 'To Ireland he was brought back in visions by the angels of God: Often was he in vision, solicited to return thither again.'

Muirchú's *Life of Patrick*, written in the seventh century, contains a prophecy that seems to foretell the coming of St Patrick to Ireland. The prophecy stated that a man with a tonsure who was passionate, wore a cloak and carried a crosier would arrive. It was predicted that people would listen to what this man preached. Such a prophecy, if indeed it had been made, would have made the ruling kings and their druid spiritual leaders nervous when Patrick came to Ireland fitting the description and gathering a following among the people.

The Hymn of Fiacc also seems to confirm such a prophecy:

The Tuatha of Erin [Ireland] were prophesying that a new kingdom of faith would come, that it would last for evermore: The land of Tara [the seat of the high king] would be waste and silent. The druids of Loegaire [the King of Tara] concealed not from him the coming of Patrick; their prophecy was verified as to the kingdom of which they spoke.

Patrick's Deeds

Patrick's other self-authored account is a letter he wrote in response to an attack on his new converts. He addressed the letter to the soldiers who had carried out the attack that killed some Christians and enslaved others. The attackers were under the authority of a British king, perhaps from Wales, named Coroticus. While not a stranger to such raids, Patrick was infuriated that Christians in particular had been targeted. Was the raid directed at him, an attempt to halt the evangelizing? Patrick says in the beginning of the letter, 'I have sworn to my God to teach the nations, even if I am held in contempt by some.'

Patrick pleads for the release of baptized prisoners and lets it be known that the evil acts perpetrated on the believers were carried out by '... the tyranny of Coroticus, who fears neither God nor his chosen priests...'

The letter was obviously aimed for a bigger audience than just the soldiers, who would have ignored it anyway, because Patrick issues this warning: 'So I earnestly entreat [all] "you holy and humble of heart". It is not lawful to seek favor from men such as these...'

Patrick goes on to offer hope to the remaining Christians. He urges them to read his words aloud so that all will hear them, even Coroticus.

What the existence of this letter tells us is that Patrick's words were indeed intended for the edification of everyone, whether Christian or not. We also know that he spoke up against injustice.

The druids may have foretold Patrick's coming (as written by Muirchú and Fiacc) but they didn't welcome it. The new movement was seen at first as an upheaval. As later scribes recorded Patrick's coming to Ireland, their views were tainted by their own personal prejudices. They may have referred to the druid class as being 'snakes' and thus the legend began that Patrick drove the snakes out of Ireland. There were no literal snakes in Ireland; there still aren't.

Another possible source of the legend involves Caoránach, the pre-Christian female monster depicted as a snake. The legend says that when this being attacked Patrick on his mountain, the holy man threw his bell and knocked her all the way to Lough Derg. Scholars note that Lough Derg is never mentioned in Patrick's own writings and neither is the mountain he allegedly climbed.

Another legend, very similar to the first, says Patrick climbed to the top of Eagle Mountain and fasted there for forty days, being tempted by the devil. He defeated the devil, also known as a serpent in the biblical account of Adam and Eve. More than anything else, however, Patrick is seen as a peacemaker. He brought people together under the umbrella of God's reconciliation, while still rejecting the practices that were contrary to God's ways. This is one of the many aspects of his life that is worth imitating today.

Eagle Mountain had been a sacred place to the pagans for aeons. Located in the west of Ireland, it is now called Croagh Patrick and is an important pilgrimage site for many Christians, especially on the last Sunday in July (Reek Sunday), when tens of thousands of people climb to the mountain top – many of them barefoot – to pray and to remember and honour St Patrick. The legend says that Patrick built a church on the mountain, and in recent times a stone foundation was discovered and carbon dated back to Patrick's day.

Patrick's Legacy

Most cherished of all the writings attributed to St Patrick is a prayer. Although probably written later by a monk who was influenced by Patrick, 'St Patrick's Breastplate' is traditionally credited to Patrick. Despite its origin, it is a prayer that reveals the Celtic thought regarding God's presence and power. The title describes the prayer's call for God's protection. It is also known as 'The Lorica', a term for a hard protective shell, body armour or breastplate.

Besides leaving behind his Celtic beliefs that were included in this prayer, Patrick's legacy includes stories that go beyond entertainment to reveal how he connected the people with God. One famous legend about Patrick involves Tara, the seat of the High King of Ireland, a title that was greatly disputed. In any case, the king held a position of power. Patrick converted the Irish by way of converting the kings. Many times whole households or clans were baptized together.

The legend states that Patrick arrived near Tara on the eve of Easter. He lit a paschal fire on the Hill of Slane. In those days it was the pagan practice to put out all fires before a royal fire was ignited on the Hill of Tara. When Patrick's fire was spotted, the king's druids told him that the fire must be put out or it would never be extinguished (probably a reference to the prophecy pertaining to Patrick). The fire continued to burn. What followed was the 'Legend of the Deer's Cry', another name for 'St Patrick's Breastplate' or 'The Lorica'.

Patrick

Patrick and his followers were marching through a hostile king's territory. As they proceeded along, they recited a prayer that asked for God's protection. They were miraculously turned into a herd of deer, successfully slipping past their adversaries.

There was an ancient belief in shape shifting or the ability to turn into another creature and then back into a human state. Druids, highly revered spiritual leaders, were thought to have the ability to shape shift. If Patrick's God had given him the same ability, then the Irish would have viewed him as a Christian druid, someone with authority who deserved attention. This idea would have resonated with the pagan Irish natives Patrick sought to reach.

Offering a prayer for protection was a common practice in the pagan world. Patrick's calling on his God to protect him would have coincided with the beliefs of the ancient native Irish, earning him respect. Patrick's task then would have been to show how his God is superior to the pagan gods.

The words of 'St Patrick's Breastplate' are recorded in the ancient *Book of Armagh*, dating from the ninth century. The following extracts are from a translation of the prayer by Cecil F. Alexander in 1889.

Patrick wished his followers to take on the protection of the triune God and therefore be free to encounter and face all dangers with confidence. The opening lines of the prayer reflects Patrick's leading:

> *I bind unto myself today*
> *The strong Name of the Trinity*

Patrick's followers could use this verse to testify to their faith and to keep God's word, his angels and his people close to their hearts:

> *I bind unto myself the power*
> *Of the great love of cherubim;*
> *The sweet 'Well done' in judgment hour,*
> *The service of the seraphim,*

Confessors' faith, Apostles' word,
The Patriarchs' prayers, the prophets' scrolls...

By observing God's creation, and the glory and power displayed daily, the ancient Irish Christians were constantly reminded of the greatness and majesty of God:

The virtues of the star lit heaven,
The glorious sun's life giving ray,
The whiteness of the moon at even,
The flashing of the lighting free,
The whirling wind's tempestuous shocks,
The stable earth, the deep salt sea
Around the old eternal rocks.

Patrick's followers trusted God and his mighty angels to protect them from physical harm and destructive words from others and from the wrongful desires of their own wayward hearts:

His heavenly host to be my guard.
Against the demon snares of sin,
The vice that gives temptation force,
The natural lusts that war within,
The hostile men that mar my course...

Against their fierce hostility
I bind to me these holy powers.
Against all Satan's spells and wiles,
Against false words of heresy,
Against the knowledge that defiles,
Against the heart's idolatry,
Against the wizard's evil craft...

The child of God can fear no ill,
his chosen dread no foe;
we leave our fate with thee, and wait
thy bidding when to go.
'Tis not from chance our comfort springs,
thou art our trust, O King of kings.

ATTRIBUTED TO ST COLUMBA

22

The oft-quoted section below is reflective of Patrick's own words in his *Confession*, when he described God's voice as 'within me or beside me' and 'above me'. It is a description of the omnipresent God, one that is never far away from us:

> *Christ be with me, Christ within me,*
> *Christ behind me, Christ before me,*
> *Christ beside me, Christ to win me,*
> *Christ to comfort and restore me.*
> *Christ beneath me, Christ above me,*
> *Christ in quiet, Christ in danger,*
> *Christ in hearts of all that love me,*
> *Christ in mouth of friend and stranger.*

Patrick's legacy lives on. If you travel to Ireland today you can visit some of the places associated with Patrick, such as Armagh, which has been recognized as an important church centre since the Middle Ages. From here we get many of the stories about St Patrick. By the eighth century, when the monastic churches overtook Ireland, Armagh sought to legitimize its claim to oversee a number of monasteries by promoting its connection to St Patrick. One of its clergy, Muirchú, in his *Life of Patrick*, described the saint as a conquering hero, in contrast to the rather humble way Patrick described himself in his *Confession* and his letter to Coroticus. Despite Patrick never mentioning Armagh in his own writings, Muirchú claimed that Armagh was the centre of all Patrick's missionary work.

The book also gives a version of the paschal fire story, but this time Patrick retaliates against the king's druids with great feats, and wins every contest, thus proving that Patrick's God is more powerful than the druids' gods. Muirchú claims that he referenced a book by Ultán (a sixth-century abbot-bishop), which does not survive, and he also likely relied on oral traditions, so it would not be accurate to assume that Muirchú had no basis for his stories. However, it's clear that Muirchú was politically motivated when he extolled Patrick's influence. In any case, the book is written in an entertaining, fictional style. Without others' accounts bringing attention to Patrick the world may have missed his story altogether.

According to *The Hymn of Fiacc*, Patrick received his last communion from a follower of his called Tassach. The ruins of St Tassach's Church can still be seen in Raholp, near Saul. It was in Saul that Patrick is said to have first preached in Ireland, and a reconstructed church with a round tower stands there. It's also said that Patrick founded a church in a barn in Saul, which is just 2 miles away from Downpatrick and the traditional burial place of Patrick at Down Cathedral. There, it is believed, the remains of the three patron saints were interred in the twelfth century.

It's interesting that all parts of Ireland claim Patrick as their guiding saint, from the north where he is buried to the west where his famous mountain lies, and all parts in between. He spread the Christian faith throughout Ireland, and thus is honoured and celebrated by both Catholics and Protestants.

As he brought new faith to Ireland so may he bring to you, a touch of Irish happiness in everything you do; and like the good St Patrick may your home and life be blessed, with all God's special favours which make you happiest.

OLD IRISH BLESSING

BRIGID

As sun shineth among stars, (so) will shine the maiden's deeds and merits.
FROM *ON THE LIFE OF ST BRIGIT*

Brigid's Life

Brigid lived from approximately 451 to 525. No figure is more revered in Ireland with as much controversy surrounding the question of her existence than Brigid (also spelled Bride, Brigit, Brighid, Bridget). There was a popular pagan goddess named Brigid (which translates to 'exalted one'), and some of her attributes were assigned to the Christian who became St Brigid when Christianity took over the island. We have no writings from Brigid and no contemporary accounts of her life. Despite the shadow of doubt this casts over Brigid's life, people in Ireland and in many other places in the world cherish her. What we do have is stories – lots of stories about her deeds and merits. It's not surprising that all we have is what has been passed down orally; as is the case with most old legends the ancient texts that refer to Brigid were transcribed oral tales, perhaps at times embellished by the author. They were only recorded on vellum after many generations had recited them in tales and ballads.

There are two well-known ancient biographies of Brigid: *The Life of St Brigit the Virgin*, by the seventh-century scribe Cogitosus, a monk at Kildare, the site of Brigid's dual monastery; and *Beatha Bhrighdi (The Life of Brigid)* in the *Leabhar Breac (The Speckled Book)*, dating to the fifteenth century. Other accounts of her life were written, which sometimes contradict each other. The stories they contain are so fanciful that Joseph A. Knowles, writing in his *St Brigid, Patroness of Ireland*, felt compelled to offer this caution to readers of the ancient works on Brigid:

> *In a life of the Saint... many legends and traditions must be introduced to stimulate the devotion of the reader, and to relieve the monotony which would inevitably ensue from a mere studied recital of historical detail.*

He goes on to quote a translator who urged that the stories be read with an understanding of the mindset and traditions of the ancient people.

It is certain, however, that Brigid was highly esteemed. One ancient account is proof: 'With Patrick, the pre-eminent, she is a pillar of the kingdom, the helper of helpers, the Queen of Queens' (from the scribe Colgan, attributed to St Columba). Another ancient source extols her: 'In our island of Hibernia Christ was made known to man by the very great miracles which he performed through the happy virgin of celestial life, famous for her merits through the whole world' (*St Ultan's Hymn*).

Brigid was born to Dubthach, a man of some wealth who owned a dairy, and his slave girl, Broicsech. Dubthach's wife was none too happy and urged him to send the pregnant thrall far away. He sold her to a druid but did not

26

sell the unborn child. Shrewd as he was, he listened to advisors and would not part with two slaves for the price of one. When the child was old enough, she returned to Dubthach's household.

There were many prophecies about the unborn child and how special she would be. Even the manner of her birth was predicted. From the *Leabhar Breac*: 'The prophet said that the child that would be brought forth on the morrow at sunrise, and neither within the house nor without, shall surpass every child in Ireland.' Brigid was born the next morning when her mother fell bringing in the milk and landed on the threshold, half inside the house and half outside. It was clear from the beginning that Brigid was not to be an ordinary girl.

One of the earliest tales involves fire, and this is where some believe the saint and goddess converge, because fire is closely associated with the goddess Brigid. But fire also has meaning in the Christian faith. According to the *Leabhar Breac*:

> On a certain day the bondmaid went to her island, and covered up her daughter in her house. Certain neighbours saw the house wherein the girl was all ablaze, so that a flame of fire was made of it from earth to heaven. But when they went to rescue the house, the fire appeared not, and this they said, that the girl was full of the grace of the Holy Spirit.

Brigid's Deeds

Fire is also involved in the legend surrounding the site of Brigid's monastery, founded late in the fifth century in Kildare (*Cill-Dara* in Irish, Church of the Oak). The site, like so many Christian sites in Ireland, was formerly sacred to the pagans – a shrine to the goddess Brigid. It is said that the sisters tended a continuously burning fire there for centuries. In Brigid's lifetime, she and nineteen other sisters perpetuated the fire. After Brigid's death it is said that no one was needed to tend the fire on the twentieth night; it continued as if Brigid herself was tending it. The fire pit was surrounded by brush and no

Brigid

man was allowed to enter. Some sources say that in the year 1220, fearing the practice was pagan, an archbishop ordered the fire to be extinguished. It was soon relit and continued on until the Reformation, when it was smothered once again. In 1993 Mary Teresa Cullen, leader of the Brigidine Sisters, relit the fire ceremoniously at Market Square in Kildare, and it has been kept burning ever since. A thirteenth-century cathedral is built on the site where it is believed Brigid established her church, and the remains of an ancient oratory that appears to date from Brigid's era are visible. Whether or not it is the site of Brigid's original fire is unknown.

One of three patron saints of Ireland, Brigid's most endearing quality was her generosity. The old Irish saying, 'Stretch out your hand in giving and you will never stretch it out in want', certainly applied to Brigid.

At first glance Brigid's generosity doesn't seem extraordinary; plenty of people are giving, loving individuals. But taken in historical context, Brigid's giving to the poor was significant. She lived during the time the Roman empire fell and Western Europe was in upheaval. A reasonable assumption is that refugees came to Ireland – displaced people who had no livelihood and who had fled the barbarian invasions that had resulted when there was no Roman army in place. The only way to survive in Ireland during that tumultuous time was to be connected to a clan or a royal family, either as a member or as a slave. Without that, people were forced to wander the wilderness and feed themselves as best they could. Even those who had food to eat would not have had plenty; so, to give away something might mean one's own demise.

It is against this impoverished background that Brigid stands out as a remarkable figure: she gave away her father's milk, his butter, even his cherished possessions. Not surprisingly, her father sought to be rid of her, as seen in this tale.

Convinced that the best thing was to sell his daughter into service to the king, Dubthach took Brigid in his chariot and travelled to the castle. He bid her to stay put outside while he enquired of the king. While he was gone, a beggar

happened by. Being away from the dairy, the supply of food from which she had
fed the poor, Brigid searched for something to give the poor man and spotted the
gleam of metal in the sun. She pulled out her father's sword from beneath some
blankets. It was not an ordinary sword, but one with a jewel-encrusted hilt.
Just as she was handing it over to the beggar, her father returned with the king.
Dubthach declared that this was just the reason he had to be rid of her.

The king, being as wise as his position required, asked Brigid whether,
if she were to be under his authority, she would give away his cattle and
possessions. Brigid answered truthfully. If she had all the wealth of the King
of Leinster, she would give it away to the poor in the name of God. The king
was humbled by this reply and told her father that she was far nobler than
either of them. He gave Dubthach a sword to replace the one given away and
granted Brigid her freedom.

By giving to others Brigid gave to her God. She is said to have believed that
Christ was in the poor person, a belief held by all the Celtic Christians. They
gave freely and without reservation as though giving to the Lord.

Brigid was always rewarded because neither she nor the owner of the
goods was ever in need: the more she gave away, the more she had to give. The
cows always had more milk to give, no matter how many times she milked
them; there was always more butter in the crock. This never-ending supply of
blessings was one of the great miraculous abilities attributed to her.

One story goes that as she was making butter for a druid, she piled up
twelve equal mounds with an additional mound in the centre. The centre
portion was larger than the others. The druid asked if she intended to keep
the big portion for herself. She denied it, saying that the twelve portions
represented the twelve disciples of Christ and the largest pile, Christ himself. It
was that portion she intended to give away.

Later, when Brigid was determined to become a nun, she went to receive
the veil from Bishop Macaille (or Mel). The bishop witnessed a pillar of fire on

*Whether my house is dark or bright, I close
it not on any wight, lest Thou, hereafter, King of
Stars, against me close Thy Heavenly bars. If
from a guest who shares thy board Thy dearest dainty
thou shalt hoard, 'tis not that guest, O never doubt it, but
Mary's Son shall do without it.*

FROM *THE CELTIC PSALTERY* BY ALFRED PERCEVAL GRAVES

Brigid's head and consecrated her a bishop, saying that it was no mistake; it was what God had willed. This story endears Brigid to many women because she, in addition to being kind and giving, became a leader in the church. It's not as remarkable, however, as it sounds. Women in ancient Ireland often held positions of power and influence, and probably in Brigid's day no one in Ireland would have given it a second thought.

There is a male bishop associated with Brigid. Conleth was a recluse and lived near the River Liffey. When Brigid set up her community, the old man came to visit her. His chariot had a faulty wheel, and with his rig in such a state he couldn't return home. Brigid said a blessing on both Bishop Conleth and his chariot driver. They were able to continue on their way, although it should not have been possible on a wheel without an axle.

Some accounts say that Brigid and Conleth remained friends and she invited him to perform the duties of bishop at Kildare when needed. She may even have invited him to help oversee her dual monastery, thus ending his hermitage. Since he lived nearby, they probably did have some kind of arrangement. What help she needed, if indeed she had been consecrated a bishop, is not clear. A monastery filled with a large number of both men and women may have required an administrator of each sex.

Brigid's Legacy

The concept of *anamcara* (also spelled *anamchara*), or soul friend, is deeply spiritual. Without an *anamcara*, one is lost, and this idea is expressed by the belief that Brigid had once said that a person without an *anamcara* is like a body without a head. Friendship fulfils the human longing to be loved and understood. Brigid may have had many different *anamchairde* during her long lifetime, and it's reasonable to conclude that Bishop Conleth served in that role.

Later, this requirement would be written into the monastic rules (religious codes of practice) of St Columba: 'a few religious men to converse with thee of

God and his Testament; to visit thee on days of solemnity; to strengthen thee in the Testaments of God, and the narratives of the Scriptures'. And also into the rule of Carthage, paraphrased here: 'If you are an *anamcara* to another, do not barter his soul; don't be blind and lead the blind; don't let his soul fall away.'

Long before the Christian era the Irish embraced the concept of close friendship. An old Irish blessing proclaimed the importance of friendship: 'You should be poor in misfortune. You should be rich in blessings. You should be slow to make enemies and quick to make friends.' Whether in battle or in the farm field, the Irish felt the need to depend on each other. Perhaps the spirit of God, in the intimacy of the trinity, inspired them before they knew his name.

Brigid cared deeply for people and wished that she could not only provide for them and see them happy, but also do the same for Christ and his heavenly hosts. This attribute was what Lady Gregory, a late-nineteenth-century Irish folklorist, translated from ancient texts when she said:

These were the wishes of Brigit: 'I would wish a great lake of ale for the King of Kings; I would wish the family of Heaven to be drinking it through life and time. I would wish the men of Heaven in my own house; I would wish vessels of peace to be given to them.'

Brigid is especially revered in matters of housekeeping. Like the keeper of the house whose job it is to nurture and care for the family who lives there, Brigid is remembered as a protector and provider. Down through the ages women tending their fires at the end of the day so that a spark would be left in which to light the new day's fire would speak her name:

I save this fire as Christ saved everyone; Brigit beneath it, the Son of Mary within it; let the three angels having most power in the court of grace be keeping this house and the people of this house and sheltering them until the dawn of day.

TRANSLATED BY LADY GREGORY

Brigid

Another from Alfred Perceval Graves:

Let us preserve this seed of fire as Christ preserves us all: Himself a-watch above the house, Bride at its middle wall, below the Twelve Apostles of highest heavenly sway, guarding and defending it until the dawn of day.

The Feast of St Brigid (1 February) celebrates the first day of spring, or the Celtic festival of Imbolc, when farmers began the planting season. It is also the traditional start of the fishing season. If a hedgehog was seen on this day, mild weather was predicted. If he hurried back to his den, however, the forecast was for bad weather. This is thought to be the precursor to the American observance of Groundhog Day on 2 February.

Legend says that Brigid, known as the patron saint of farmers and dairy workers, was born on 1 February. She once wove a cross out of rushes to explain the gospel to a dying pagan. (In those days rushes were spread on the floor for comfort.) In some parts of Ireland children weave the crosses on the eve of the Feast of St Brigid and distribute them to their neighbours. Each year a fresh cross is hung over the doors of homes and barns or placed in the rafters in remembrance of the story and to ask God's blessing and protection.

Historically, in some places the old crosses were destroyed or hung elsewhere in the house, but in many places they remained in the rafters and the age of the house could be determined by counting the crosses.

There are many variations of Brigid's cross throughout of Ireland. Some say that the four sections of the cross represent the seasons of the sun and the Celtic festivals of Lughnasa, Samhain, Imbolc and Beltane, and others see in the cross a wheel representing the continuous cycle of life. While those things are significant, Christians remember the story about Brigid weaving the cross to carry the message of salvation. Brigid's cross reminds us of the incredible self-sacrifice of one of God's earliest missionaries. Today crosses are hung in

34

homes to ask God to bless and protect the occupants the way that he, through Brigid, blessed and protected those she encountered.

One remarkable high cross's ornamentation is reminiscent of the diamond shape of the traditional St Brigid's cross. While other high crosses contain the design, the best example is probably the twelfth-century High Cross of Dysert O'Dea in County Clare, with its five-diamond design on the centre of one face of the cross.

As part of the celebration of St Brigid's Day, the Irish would make fresh butter (Brigid was a dairymaid) and place it outside on the windowsill along with bread and a bit of corn for her cow. Brigid is also known for possessing a rare red-eared cow, an indication of her importance. The idea behind leaving these things was the hope that St Brigid would pass by and bless the harvest and household. In honour of the memory of Brigid's generosity people would sometimes give away the butter and bread to a needy family.

In some parts of Ireland the eldest daughter in a family, or another designated family member, would role-play as the saint and knock on the front door. She would say in Irish Gaelic: 'Go down on your knees, do homage and let blessed Brigid enter the house.' The appropriate response would be: 'O, Come in, you are a hundred times welcome.'

Similarly in some parts of Ireland and Scotland ribbons or garments were draped over bushes and tree branches on the eve of St Brigid's Day in the hope that Brigid would bless them. This is in remembrance of Brigid's mantle (cloak), about which another wonderful story is told.

Brigid was in need of some land for her monastery. She went to the King of Leinster and asked for only as much land as her mantle would cover. This seemed like a small request to the king who realized that she could have asked for much more. He quickly agreed. When Brigid began to spread out her cloak, a miracle occurred. Before the garment could touch the ground it grew and expanded, covering mile after mile of territory until the king pleaded with her to make it stop, fearing he'd lose all his kingdom because he could not go back on his word. As a result Brigid received a fine piece of land upon which to build. Even today, garments are draped on tree branches and bushes on the eve of St Brigid's Day, to wish for a blessing.

Brigid's example is one of charity and nurturing. Her remarkable life has never been forgotten although more than a millennium separates her life from ours today. A good deed is never forgotten. Many good deeds result in a legacy.

Sweet heaven's smile
Gleamed o'er the Isle,
That gems the dreary sea,
One far gone day,
And flash'd its ray,
More than a thousand years away,
Pure Bridget, over thee.

REV. ABRAM J. RYAN, FROM *ST BRIGID, PATRONESS OF IRELAND*, TRANSLATED BY JOSEPH A. KNOWLES

COLUMCILLE

Alone with none but Thee, my God,
I journey on my way;
What need I fear when Thou art near,
Oh King of night and day?
More safe am I within Thy hand
Than if a host did round me stand.

ATTRIBUTED TO ST COLUMBA

Columcille's Life

One of Ireland's three patron saints, Columcille (also spelled Colm Cill or, in the Roman fashion, Columba), whose name means Dove of the Church, came from the powerful O'Neill clan. He lived from approximately 521 to 597. He was descended from Niall of the Nine

> *That I might search the books all,*
> *That would be good for my soul;*
> *At times kneeling to beloved Heaven;*
> *At times contemplating the King of Heaven,*
> *Holy the chief;*
> *At times at work without compulsion,*
> *This would be delightful.*
>
> ATTRIBUTED TO ST COLUMBA

Hostages, the king that was probably responsible for the raid that brought Patrick to Ireland as a slave. Columcille was wealthy and privileged, presumably in line to be High King had he not chosen the religious life. He journeyed to Gaul reportedly to visit the tomb of St Martin of Tours, and in spite of his royal and perhaps pampered background he became a monk. After studying with several different teachers, Columcille became a student of Finian at Clonard. Finian was an exceptional teacher but one who expected his charges to lead a harsh life of discipline and sacrifice.

Columcille's Deeds

Columcille founded many monasteries in northern Ireland, and proved himself as not only a leader but also a poet, a position that was highly regarded in ancient Ireland.

Columcille was a protector of nature, choosing to build his churches in such a way that would cut down as few of the beloved oak trees as possible. He also had a fondness for books, which in those days were extremely valuable possessions. Under the cover of darkness, without so much as a candle because, according to legend, his fingers were luminous, Columcille copied a Psalter belonging to a different Finian, Finian of Moville.

An old Irish saying declares that 'All sins cast long shadows', and it was true that Columcille could not hide what he had done. His deceit was uncovered and it was considered a major offence. By copying a book the original lost its unique value. The case was brought before King Diarmait, a rival of Columcille's clansmen, who rendered the following judgment: 'To every cow her calf; to every book its copy.' Columcille had to return his copy to Finian.

Ancient Ireland saw many tribal feuds and wars. Columcille belonged to the most powerful family in Ireland at that time, and they had no hesitation in defending their rank with force. He seized an opportunity

38

for revenge because of some wrong supposedly committed by Diarmait.
The king may have issued an order to kill one of Columcille's monks
or someone else who had taken sanctuary at Columcille's monastery.
Believing that this death had to be avenged, Columcille called upon the
armies of his clan, which ultimately outmatched those of Diarmait. The
battle of Cooldrevny (in Sligo) in 561 was a massacre. Three thousand of
Diarmait's warriors were slaughtered while Columcille's army lost only
one. As a result, Columcille received his coveted book, but at a great price.
Columcille's beloved book was for centuries carried into battle by those
who believed it had protective powers and was called *Cathach*, or 'Battler'.
An ancient book by that title is held today by the Royal Irish Academy,
after having been rediscovered in the seventeenth century, and is dated
to Columcille's day. There is no conclusive proof that this book is the very
one Columcille penned, but the incomplete manuscript contains Psalms
30:10 to 105:13 in the Vulgate (St Jerome's translation dating from
the fourth century), and some go so far as to say the text appears to be
hurriedly written.

Some accounts say that Columcille imposed his own punishment for
what he had done, while others say his confessor issued the penalty for
Columcille's unholy behaviour. He was banished from his homeland, or
else he went willingly, and was told to convert 3,000 souls to Christianity,
the number of deaths that his war over a book had caused.

Iona, an island just north of the pagan land of the Picts, or Alban
(modern-day Scotland), was chosen because Columcille's beloved
Ireland could not be seen from its shores. Poems attributed to Columcille
illustrate his love for his homeland, especially Derry, where he founded a
monastery.

The miniscule island of Iona is just over 3 miles long and less than
2 miles wide. Columcille travelled there with twelve other monks. This

The reason I love Derry is for its quietness,
for its purity, for its crowds of white angels.
ATTRIBUTED TO COLUMCILLE

custom of symbolizing Jesus and his twelve disciples on important journeys carried many monks abroad in the sixth century, although sometimes larger numbers travelled together.

Along with being known for possessing a gift of prophecy and for his wisdom, Columcille is credited with many miracles, just like all the saints of old. One famous story linked with the saint is the legend of the Loch Ness monster. It seems Columcille approached the River Ness just as some people were burying a man who had been killed by a monster in the river. Columcille ordered one of his men to swim across the river to procure a boat on the other side. Bravely, the man agreed, but just as he reached the middle of the stream the monster reappeared and tried to eat him. Columcille raised his hand in the air, made the sign of the cross and ordered the monster to halt, which it miraculously did, dangerously close to the swimmer. Furthermore, Columcille declared that the creature would never leave that place, the stream that feeds the lake called Loch Ness. The monster dove back to the riverbed and the man continued on, got the boat and returned to Columcille. All the witnesses, some of whom were not Christian, praised the God of Columcille for this act.

Columcille did return to Ireland. He was beckoned to attend a convention in Derry of noblemen, scholars and clergy, the purpose of which was to address the matter of poets in Ireland. Their influence had threatened the kings; they were becoming something of a nuisance and were in danger of being banned. Columcille could not sit back and see this happen. He was a poet too and did not want the occupation prohibited in Ireland. To avoid breaching the terms of his exile he made the trip blindfolded. There was a massive frenzy at the return of the exiled abbot, who was hailed as a returning hero. He addressed the group so convincingly, extolling the merits of preserving the ancient art, that

Columcille

the matter was resolved satisfactorily, and he returned to Iona having completed a successful mission.

Columcille was well known and respected for his vast influence in his own day. He is said to have continued transcribing almost until his final breath. According to *The Life of Columba* written by Adamnán, an abbot of Iona, Columcille predicted his own death. Adamnán describes how his faithful horse wept for him on his last day of life. The Dove of the Church blessed his monastery, saying:

Small and mean though this place is, yet it shall be held in great and unusual honour, not only by Scotic [Irish] kings and people, but also by the rulers of foreign and barbarous nations, and by their subjects; the saints also even of other churches shall regard it with no common reverence.

He returned to his cell and proceeded to copy Psalm 34. Too frail to continue, he declared that a fellow monk should finish it. The last words he wrote were 'The lions may grow weak and hungry, but those who seek the Lord lack no

good thing' (Psalm 34:10). He then joined his brothers for vespers, following which he went to his bed, laid his head on his pillow (a stone) and said to his attendants:

> ... be at peace, and have unfeigned charity among yourselves; and if you thus follow the example of the holy fathers, God, the Comforter of the good, will be your Helper and I, abiding with Him, will intercede for you; and He will not only give you sufficient to supply the wants of this present life, but will also bestow on you the good and eternal rewards which are laid up for those that keep His commandments.

Surprisingly, this was not to be his last act. When the bell tolled at midnight for prayers, he rose from his bed with renewed vigour. He arrived at the church before the others and when they followed they saw a great light coming from the altar at which Columcille knelt. The light illuminated the entire building. Then suddenly all went black, and the monks stumbled around in the darkness until they found their beloved abbot. They held up his

Columcille

right hand, and Columcille silently blessed them before taking his last breath. The witnesses said that his face was aglow as though he saw the angels that seemed to have surrounded him his entire life.

Columcille's Legacy

With historical perspective one can see why Columcille was such a consequential figure. Rome, since most of the army had been pulled out and moved to its Eastern empire, was in the process of disintegration. Entire portions of Europe had been conquered by invaders. The remaining Christian church functioned within its boundaries but was isolated. In Ireland monasteries were flourishing and monks were copying manuscripts with passion.

When Columcille left Ireland, he and his successors took the Christian faith, and its written history, to pagan-dominated Europe. Irish monks identified three types of martyrdom: red martyrdom (when one gives up his life); white martyrdom (when one gives up comforts and all familiar surroundings to commit himself completely to God) and green martyrdom (as distinct from the white martyrdom of the Egyptian monks who retreated to the 'white' deserts, the green signifying the lush islands and forests of Ireland). Columcille's 'green martyrdom', as it was called, involved a pilgrimage into the unknown, for he could not have understood at the time how important his move would be.

Just as there were Christians in Ireland before Patrick's arrival, there were Christians in Scotland before Columcille landed. But the measure of his influence in spreading the faith is significant. Columcille, with his princely background and his unwillingness to accept defeat, established a Christian order that endured and expanded, sending out even more great missionaries.

*He knew seasons and storms; he read the secrets of the great wisdom;
he knew the course of the moon; he took notice of its race with the
branching sun. He was skilful in the course of the sea; to tell every high
thing we have heard from Colum, would be to count the stars of heaven.*

FORGAILL, CHIEF POET OF IRELAND, SPEAKING OF COLUMCILLE. FROM *THE KILTARTAN POETRY BOOK*, BY

LADY GREGORY

Columcille

THE APOSTLES OF ERIN

Get all the advice and instruction you can,
so you will be wise the rest of your life.

PROVERBS 19:20

Early Monasticism

Monasteries in ancient Ireland were not quite what they are today. They consisted of a series of small wooden buildings and a church surrounded by a raised circle of earth or a rampart called a rath. Some were bordered by a circular wall of stone called a cashel. Normally made of wood, some of the early churches were made of stone. The churches were built so that they aligned east and west, with the doorway on the west end. With time

> *For it is not by path of feet, nor by motion*
> *of body, that one draws nigh to God, but it is*
> *through practice of good customs and virtues.*
> FROM *THE LIFE OF ST COLUMBA (LEABHAR BREAC)*

they became more ornate and decorated, but scholars and archaeologists believe the earlier churches were quite plain and for the most part not large. The earliest monasteries were not associated with wealth, as they later came to be, attracting the attention of raiding Vikings.

The communities were primarily concerned with prayer, labour, study and discipline. Each cell was home to one or two monks and they ate little – just bread, water and vegetables, except on feast days and the Sabbath, when some communities allowed meat. Seeking a life of denial of worldly goods prompted one to focus on heavenly treasures.

The land around a monastery was a sanctuary. Anyone accused of wrongdoing could claim immunity there and not be immediately harmed, though he or she might later have to face judgment. A sacred grove of trees either grew or was planted in the sanctuary. As these monasteries gained importance, more and more people wanted to live there.

In Europe a bishop was associated with a city, where he presided over a diocese. Ireland had no cities, very few roads and dense forest separating settlements. While bishops alone could consecrate new bishops and priests and were still leaders in the church hierarchy, the Roman bishopric model was ineffective in Ireland (although sometimes abbots were also bishops). Here the monasteries took on the leadership role and became small functioning centres of commerce as well as religious learning establishments, sometimes connected to each other, and other times operating independently. In Ireland there was no central authority – bishops had no say over the operation of a monastery. The Irish abbots and monks were sometimes married and raised families in their monasteries, unlike their Roman counterparts. The control of the monasteries frequently passed to family members and was very often connected to royal families who contributed land for the sites. Women sometimes served as abbesses and were not segregated into convents.

The Fathers of Monasticism

The early stages of Irish Christianity developed into a monastic movement in the sixth century. Two men were given the title 'Father of Monasticism' because of their influence. From them stems the great movement that both nurtured the Christian faith in Ireland and restored it to many parts of Europe where it had been lost.

St Finian

Around the year 520 an Irish monk named Finian established a centre of learning that would have a profound effect. Finian was no ordinary monk. He was extremely well trained, having been schooled at St Martin of Tours in Gaul and in several monasteries in Wales. He took well to the rigours of monastic life and studied hard, seeking God's way. He returned to Ireland and continued his study, as the legend goes, with Brigid at Kildare. From there he established his school at Cluain Eraird (Clonard), apparently originally intended to be his own small retreat. Word travelled, and those seeking spiritual guidance journeyed to Finian's home. It's hard to imagine why so many would choose to live like Finian – sleeping on a cold floor with a stone for a pillow, forsaking all physical comforts – but the desire to find one's significance in the eyes of God was great.

The site of Finian's centre of learning was an area along the banks of the beautiful River Boyne in the abundant meadowland long thought to be spiritually significant. The school became a magnet for the pursuit of knowledge and the pursuit of God. The monastic centre once housed as many as 3,000 people. Some of the most eminent fathers of the Irish church were educated there.

St Enda

Many future apostles of Erin (Ireland) also studied under St Enda on the Aran Islands off the west coast of Ireland. Brendan the Navigator is said to have consulted with Enda before leaving on his famous journey, and Columcille may have travelled to Aran to discover Enda's wisdom. Even St Finian may have consulted Enda. A former warrior, Enda turned to the priesthood after suffering a broken heart. He built churches at Drogheda on the east coast of Ireland, but his most famous monasteries were built on property given to him by the King of Cashel on the Aran Islands. Because his community was among the earliest in Ireland – if not the earliest – and because many respected Irish monks studied under Enda, he shares the title 'Father of Monasticism' with Finian of Clonard. Enda's example of finding a lonely place to serve God was a major influence on those who came after him.

Twelve Who Made a Difference

Jesus' apostles spread the Christian message beyond their homeland. And so it was with the men who are called the Twelve Apostles of Erin, clerics who were all thought to have studied at Clonard. Some are well known and celebrated; others we know little about. Taken together this group formed the springboard from which the Irish Celtic way of Christianity was launched.

St Ciaran of Saighir (Seir-Kieran)

The appearance of this fifth-century bishop's name in the list is a little surprising. He was Bishop of Ossory in Munster and is probably included because he is sometimes called the 'first saint of Ireland'. In reality he preceded the founding of Clonard. He may have been one of the Christians known to have been in Ireland before Patrick's arrival or was at least Patrick's contemporary. Legend says that Ciaran met Patrick in Britain where Patrick gave him a bell. He was to return to Ireland, carrying the bell. Wherever the bell rang, that would be the place where he was to build his church. Though an interesting legend, it is unlikely since Ciaran would have been Patrick's senior and probably was not seeking guidance from a young former slave.

The monastery at Grangefertagh (shortened to Fertagh) in County Kilkenny is the probable site of Ciaran's monastery. A round tower there is said to date from the sixth century, but some date it earlier and believe that it was an original part of Ciaran's pre-Patrick monastery.

St Ciaran of Clonmacnoise

Not to be confused with the previous St Ciaran, this saint is the founder of Clonmacnoise, an important monastic centre. As a student he is said to have been so generous that he gave away his only book to new arrivals at the monastery in Clonard and did not complete his own studies on time because of it. He is one of the few famous monks without a royal heritage. His father was a tradesman, possibly a carpenter or a chariot-maker. He was often told that because of his common background his sacrifice to a life of devotion was not as significant as that of others who had given up a royal inheritance. Once, when he visited St Enda on Aran, he had a vision of a great tree growing in the middle of Ireland with branches spreading to all four corners of the land. Enda believed that this meant that Ciaran would be that tree of great influence, and he was, in a matter of speaking, by founding Clonmacnoise. Ciaran even set up a special section in his monastery where girls – including slaves – could live and be educated. He died young but left a legacy, and his order was maintained for centuries, reaching many who, like him, had no royal heritage.

St Brendan of Birr

He is the founder of Birr in central Ireland and a friend of the more famous St Columcille. From his monastery came the *Gospels of MacRegal*, a ninth-century book, so we know his school lasted at least that long. It is

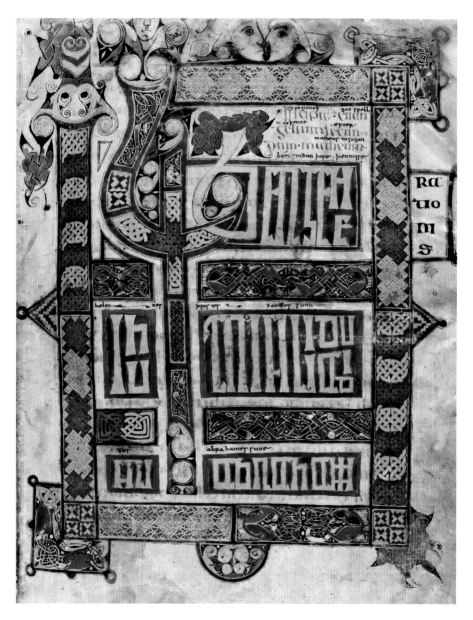

The Apostles of Erin

49

said that Columcille foresaw his friend's death and that he was carried to heaven by angels.

St Brendan of Clonfert

This founder of many monasteries was best known as Brendan the Navigator because of his illustrious journey to the west. He was in pursuit of *Tir-na-n-Og*, the Land of the Young, a fabled island spoken of since pre-Christian times. In the Middle Ages Brendan the Navigator's story was translated into many languages and was told all over Europe.

Even Christopher Columbus, before making his famous 'discovery of America' in the fifteenth century, is said to have sought out navigation advice from the Irish, and he included Irishmen in his crew. Some believe that Brendan's journey, in the sixth century, actually took the Irish monks to the North American shore, and because of a re-created excursion by adventurer Tim Severin in the 1970s, we now know it was feasible, though it has not been proven.

Along with the many miracles of raising people from the dead, predicting various events and providing food – events common in all the lives of the Irish saints written by monks – St Brendan's life includes a voyage that is filled with wonder. The story, *Navigatio Sancti Brendani*, a ninth- or tenth-century account written by an Irish monk, evokes the longing to be a *peregrini pro Christi*, a wanderer for Christ. *Peregrinatio*, or pilgrimage, is a concept that the ancient Irish Christians used to describe the spiritual journey of growing closer to God. Such a pilgrimage is an adventure, a quest, a discovery. For the *peregrini pro Christi*, this quest was a journey to pursue God and to strive for the closeness that was once experienced in the Garden of Eden before sin entered the world. It's a journey that never ends this side of heaven.

While Columcille went to the east, where there had been trade exchange and contact for generations, Brendan wandered to the unknown reaches of the west and north. And in those faraway places he witnessed wonders that he and his monks later reported to people who themselves had never strayed so far from civilization. There were enormous sea monsters, an island of crystal, islands completely covered by sheep and birds, and strange people with strange customs.

One story is that on Easter his monks stepped out on to an island to light a fire while Brendan stayed in the boat to pray. Oddly, there was no grass on the island. As the fire smouldered and then burned, the island began to move and shake. It wasn't a rock in the ocean after all but the back of a whale, and the terrified monks leapt back into the boat. According to the legend, this happened every Easter for seven years. The whale willingly lent himself to the monks for the glory of God.

Also on this journey it's said that Brendan encountered Judas who lamented his betrayal of Jesus and described the horrors of hell. Brendan was able to give Judas a respite from hell, but only for one day.

Even the waters, sometimes ice-filled, sometimes thick and still, were peculiar and unfathomable to the medieval mind, as Brendan and his monks sailed in a rudderless oxen-skin boat along what was probably the stepping stone route across the North Atlantic: Ireland, the Hebrides, the Faroes, Iceland, Greenland, Newfoundland.

The point of the story was not the physical journey, although that made for good entertainment and the story contains a great deal more concrete details and clues than most of the ancient saint narratives. Even so, the spiritual journey was much more important, as it was to all the ancients who sought to be a wanderer for Christ. To be so obedient, so trusting, as to send yourself out into the unknown, is to stretch the bounds of security so that all you can do is depend on God. When that is done, there is such a sense of peace and joy that the whole journey of hardships and wonder has been more worthwhile than can be measured.

Tears make the harvest of the heart to grow,
And love, though human, is almost divine.
The heart that loves not knows not how to pray;
The eye can never smile that never weeps:
'Tis through our sighs Hope's kindling sunbeams play,
And through our tears the bow of Promise peeps.
FROM 'THE VOYAGE OF ST BRENDAN' BY DENIS FLORENCE MACCARTHY

Colman, a follower of St Brendan the Navigator, was a poet with many years' training. During the plague outbreak of the mid-seventh century, he and his companions fled to an island off the coast near Cork. They sought refuge beyond the ninth wave of the sea, where it was believed that the plague could not travel. (An ancient belief states that the ninth wave of the sea is the most powerful; if you can defeat it and survive, then you can survive anything.) Colman composed a poem or a hymn to ask for God's protection from the plague, part of which reads:

The blessing of God come upon us. May the son of Mary cover us. May he protect us this night, wherever we go through out great numbers. Whether at rest or at motion, at sitting or standing, the King of Heaven be against every assault. This is the supplication that we offer up.

Legend says that as they were travelling to the island one of the brothers asked Colman what blessing would await them there. He replied by asking, 'What blessing is needed besides God's blessing?'

The hymn also asks for safe passage, not just on this journey but also on the greater journey awaiting us all: 'May it be true, O Lord, that it become true, that we all reach the peace of the King, that wherever we go, or arrive, we may reach the Kingdom of Heaven.'

Voyage is the theme whenever we think of Brendan or anyone connected to him. But perhaps more important is that Brendan founded Clonfert in County Galway, a booming monastery that lasted a millennium. Before his great voyage, Brendan set up monasteries all along the River Shannon and the west coast of Ireland and even across the Irish Sea in Scotland and in Wales. He also established a convent that was headed by his sister Briga.

The remains of a sixth-century stone cell on Mount Brandon, on the Dingle peninsula, suggest that this site is or is near the place that Brendan once lived. Brendan is thought to have spent a lot of time on that mountain contemplating God's will for his life. Mount Brandon is often cloud-covered, but when the sun peeks through, good weather is predicted. The mountain, the second highest in Ireland, is a sacred site and a wonder for nature lovers.

Brendan and his followers founded other monasteries as well and planted the seeds of faith that sprung to life on the Shetland and Orkney Islands off the coast of Scotland; the Faroe Islands, part of present-day Denmark; and Iceland. And of course, according to legend, on the North American continent also.

St Patrick supposedly predicted Brendan's future influence when he said that a star of the Western world would be born in west Munster. While there is no proof the patron saint ever said such a thing, the stories about Brendan did bring him fame both in the Western world and in his own country.

St Columba of Tir-da-glasí (Terryglass)

The founder of Terryglass, he supposedly visited Tours (modern-day France) and brought back relics of St Martin, a bishop born in the late fourth century who was highly venerated. He had the duty of caring for his master, St Finian, as he lay dying of plague. The Yellow Plague claimed tens of thousands across Europe, and wiped out a third of Ireland's population. As trade flourished, so did the pandemic, not sparing the rich or devoted. Plague would later take this Columba's life and also the life of another of the Twelve Apostles of Erin, Ciaran of Clonmacnoise.

St Columba of Iona

The founder of many monasteries, his most famous is in Iona, an island off the northern Scottish shore. This St Columba (Columcille) along with St Patrick and St Brigid is one of the three patron saints of Ireland. His story is covered in a previous chapter.

St Mobhí of Glasnevin

He set up his monastery in Glasnevin, just north of present-day Dublin, where Columcille is said to have studied for a time before leaving during the plague outbreak. The monastery continued on long after Mobhí died of plague, some sources say until the Viking raids in the eighth century destroyed it.

St Ruadhan of Lorrha

Ruadhan founded the monastery at Lorrha, in County Tipperary, which was so close to St Brendan of Birr's that they could hear each other's bells. Brendan is said to have moved his community because of it.

Ruadhan's monastery, a few centuries after Ruadhan's time, transcribed a text that is best known as the Stowe Missal, named for the library of the Duke of Buckingham, who acquired it much later. It is sometimes referred to more appropriately as the Lorrha Missal. The book is a priest's guide for a mass and also contains excerpts from the New Testament book of John. It is believed to represent sixth-century Irish church practices and is thought to be the oldest surviving Celtic mass book.

St Senan of Iniscathay (Scattery Island)

He was a generation older than Columcille and founded several churches and a monastery on Inishmore in the Aran Islands. His final settlement was his monastery at Scattery Island or Iniscathay in County Clare, where no women were allowed. However, he did found two convents and was visiting one when he died. He is buried at Iniscathay. Senan was one of the many abbots who were also bishops.

St Ninnidh the Saintly of Loch Erne

He was possibly the same St Ninnidh who was believed to have administered last rights to St Brigid. He became known as 'Ninnidh of the Clean Hand' because he encased in metal the hand that administered communion to Brigid. Perhaps he thought his hand was blessed after having touched the revered woman and he wanted to keep it from being defiled. This became his notoriety, but he, like the others, was a teacher and founder of schools. He established his monastery on an island in the beautiful Loch Erne in present-day County Fermanagh. He is said to have preached along the shores of the lake from a boat.

St Lasserian mac Nadfraech

Not much is known about this saint but his name suggests that he may have been related to Munster royalty. Aengus, son of Nadfraech, was the first Christian king of Munster, baptized by Patrick. Aengus, who is said to have endured having Patrick's crosier thrust into his foot – an accident on Patrick's part that Aengus thought was part of the baptism ritual – had many sons and daughters that he dedicated to the church, and it's possible that Lasserian was part of his family.

St Canice of Aghaboe

Canice was the son of an esteemed bard. He studied under many of the other Twelve Apostles of Ireland and also assisted St Columcille on Iona. The two were so close that Canice, while residing in Ireland, felt compelled to pray for Columcille in Iona. At that very moment Columcille, in a stormy sea with his companions, told his friends not to worry because Canice was running to his church, while wearing only one shoe, to pray for them. The legend says that Canice had jumped up from a table and hurried to church without properly dressing. Canice founded his monastery at Aghaboe, presently a village in County Laois in Ireland's midlands region.

However short or long these men's lives were their earthly purpose was fulfilled. Their paths overlapped. They studied under or with each other. Brendan the Navigator in particular seems to have been acquainted with several of the well-known Irish monks. He travelled to many of their monasteries and is said to have greatly mourned the passing of young Ciaran. He also visited Finian at Moville, who of course knew Columcille. Many more men, and even some women, could have carried this title. These are the twelve that historically have been named as students at Clonard and continued on to train even more apostles for Christ.

The Thirteenth Apostle of Erin

If a case could be made for a thirteenth Apostle of Erin, it would have to be St Columban. Columban (Columbanus in Latin) is one of the first great missionary monks to be associated with Bangor, a well-known monastery established by a former student of Finian, St Comgall. As a young man, despite the attention of adoring women and the pleas of his mother not to leave (he had to jump over her as she blocked the doorway of their house), Columban devoted his life to religious study in monasteries. He eventually ended up at Bangor, and much later he heard the call to travel to foreign lands. After receiving approval from his abbot to leave, he moved his missionary work out farther than the earlier monks had, founding monasteries in the Frankish and Italian kingdoms. The best known are Luxeuil in France and Bobbio in Italy.

Separated from Rome, the Irish Christians interpreted Christianity within their own culture. Bishops held little influence in their world. Known for his zeal, Columban angered the bishops in France and later in Italy with his Irish ways. He had little use for a bishop who would not venture outside the comforts of his town, and he readily made this known.

This was contrary to the ways of Rome, but Columban gave that no heed. As an abbot, he considered himself no less significant than the bishops in Europe. In fact, because bishops held little importance in Ireland since the time of Patrick, he probably considered himself a step above them. He even wrote letters to two different popes in his lifetime defending his Irish practices, and his tone could be considered irreverent. For instance, when writing to Pope Gregory the Great, Columban's tone is casual, as if conferring with a friend. He makes light of a previous pope, Leo the Great, by referencing an Old Testament verse (Ecclesiastes 9:4) when he says, 'a living dog is better than a dead lion' (*leo* is Latin for lion). Likewise, when he wrote to Pope Boniface IV he poked fun at another previous pope, Pope Vigilius, by asking the current pope to 'be vigilant', and he repeats the phrase often, ending with 'since perhaps he who was called Vigilant was not'. This may have been typical Irish humour, but it undoubtedly was not appreciated in the Roman church. It is unknown whether Columban received a reply to either of these letters.

Columban's growing popularity among the lay people, however, necessitated the expansion of his community. He and his followers had been living in an abandoned Roman castle given to him by the Frankish king. They soon built new buildings, and had to expand more than once. Columban brought a different kind of Christianity to the local people who had viewed the church as materialistic. These Irish monks asked nothing of them, unless of course they wished to join them as monks, and they shared the crops they grew with those who were hungry. More and more people wanted to learn about this type of Christianity.

His popularity worried the rulers, and his reluctance to accept their authority angered them, causing him to be expelled from France. Columban founded monasteries along the Rhine River and in Switzerland, offending the Roman church officials on the way. He may have understood that he ruffled feathers, but, as he said in one of his letters, 'My part was to challenge, question, ask.'

I wish, O Son of the living God, O ancient, eternal King,
For a hidden little hut in the wilderness that it may be my dwelling.
An all-grey lithe little lark to be by its side,
A clear pool to wash away sins through the grace of the Holy Spirit.
Quite near, a beautiful wood around it on every side,
To nurse many-voiced birds, hiding it with its shelter.

FROM 'THE HERMIT'S SONG'

During his exodus it's said he composed a boat song that the men chanted as they rowed: 'Endure and save yourselves for better things; O you who have suffered worse, this too shall end. Heia, men! Let the echoes resound with our heia!'

He finally found refuge in northern Italy on land granted to him by the king there. Columban desired to be in the countryside away from the cities, and so the organized church left the pagan-dominated wilderness to him. It seemed the common people were not offended by the Irish manner of Christianity, and they flocked to him, causing him to expand the confines of his monastery once again. Columban died at Bobbio in 615 and is buried there. His crypt, in the church at Bobbio, is still a pilgrimage site for Christians.

Jonas, a monk at Bangor, wrote the account of Columban's life. Jonas came to the monastery just a few years after Columban's death and he had access to first-hand accounts of the abbot's life and ministry, something that is rare in surviving saint narratives. Columban's legacy in Europe is remarkable: Luxeuil in France is credited with founding over a hundred new monasteries in France, Germany and Italy. Bobbio was an important learning centre for a millennium after Columban's death.

The Irish Spiritual Pilgrimage

These apostles did not always seek out places where converts might be found. On the contrary, many of their destinations were the loneliest spots one could imagine. Skellig Michael is an example. Eight miles off the south-west coast of Ireland, Skellig Michael is difficult to reach even today, when sea conditions sometimes make the journey unfeasible. The island (it is actually the larger of two rocky islands, but only one island was inhabited by people) is a jagged outcrop where the stone beehive huts of an early monastic settlement can still be seen by climbing 600 ancient steps. The huts are perched on vertical cliffs overlooking the ocean. The ancient community was active from the sixth to the twelfth century. Since travel could only be attempted during pleasant weather, the monks who lived there were truly cloistered. Without distractions one is left with one's own thoughts, and when all is quiet it's easier to hear the voice of God. Hermits pray, and prayer is a powerful way to care for humanity.

There is a seventh-century poem that is an apparent conversation between a monk named Marvan, who had chosen the life of a hermit, and his brother Guare, the King of Connaught. Marvan tries to explain the closeness he feels to God by being daily surrounded by nature. A portion of that poem follows:

> *What though in Kingly pleasures now*
> *Beyond all riches thou rejoice,*
> *Content am I my Saviour good*
> *Should on this wood have set my choice.*
>
> *Without one hour of war or strife*
> *Through all my life at peace I fare;*
> *Where better can I keep my tryst*
> *With our Lord Christ, O brother Guare?*

FROM *THE CELTIC PSALTERY* BY ALFRED PERCEVAL GRAVES

The king is convinced and wishes that he too could live such a life.

A life of solitude was not as romantically simple and serene as it might seem. Ireland at that time was mostly wilderness teeming with dangerous forest animals. But perhaps an even more difficult undertaking was in the quiet: in the absence of human contact, one has no choice but to face one's own shortcomings and inadequacies. Physical needs were not considered important; more energy was expended on spiritual growth. The desert monks

of Egypt, Syria and Palestine from several centuries earlier directly influenced the Irish model for hermits. While those monks sought solitude in the desert, the Irish went to the wilderness or the ocean. That is why they sometimes referred to their pilgrimage as a journey to the desert in the sea.

It was not a life for anyone who lacked commitment, endurance or preparedness. A hermit was formerly a monk who was required to undergo strict preparation and questioning before being allowed to take up this life. The Irish seemed to have preferred moving toward that life in stages, in which small groups of men led a somewhat solitary life together before moving on to complete isolation. A temporary hermitage was also a choice taken by many. To persist and not give up in the face of such harsh reality was admirable. The ancient accounts of these saints' lives are filled with stories of friendships with animals – an indication of the conquering of a life that most could not endure.

St Kevin

Kevin (Coemhghein or Coemgin in Irish) of Glendalough is a good example of an Irish hermit. Born of royal stock in 498 in Leinster, his early life is filled with stories about visits from angels. After religious training, he became a hermit and lived for seven years in Glendalough (meaning 'valley of two lakes'). Once when he was praying with arms outstretched, a blackbird built a nest in the palm of his hand. Not wanting to disturb the bird's eggs, he remained in that position until the baby birds hatched and flew away. An otter brought him fish daily and even saved Kevin's Psalter when he dropped it into one of the lakes.

Kevin is also credited with saving his ill foster son who asked for an apple. There were no apple trees nearby, but Kevin blessed some willow trees and then found apples within their branches. Kevin brought them to his foster son who recovered after eating them. It's said that the trees continued to produce apples for 400 years. Giraldus Cambrensis of Wales (also known as Gerald the Wise), writing in the twelfth century, said the trees existed in his day. Giraldus describes the fruit as being white and of an oblong shape. There is no trace of those trees today in Glendalough, but some have speculated that the trees may have been willow-leaf pear trees.

After seven years the growing number of followers who made their way to Kevin's hideaway – perhaps a hollow tree or a cave – necessitated the building of a community. Kevin only returned to his solitary life for a short interval after that, choosing instead to teach and direct his disciples. He once desired to take a pilgrimage to Rome but was advised against it because of all the disciples needing to be taught at Glendalough. He relented and stayed at home. Kevin may have preferred the solitary life, but the ancient Irish Christians were more concerned with what would better their brothers and sisters than with what they themselves desired.

Legend says that Kevin lived to be 120 years old. It is believed that the ruins of his stone cell can still be seen as can the site of his cave, which is not easily reached, lying at the edge of a mountain overlooking the upper lake. Kevin supposedly said to one of the angels who frequently visited

A man will not be found where he lives,
but rather where he loves.
OLD IRISH SAYING

him, 'O, holy messenger, it is impossible for monks to dwell in this valley surrounded by mountains, unless God assist them by his power.'

There is a a huge granite high cross dating to the twelfth century named for St Kevin at Glendalough on the site of the sixth-century monastery. Perhaps because of the blackbird legend, pilgrims try to wrap their arms around the cross and some say those that do will receive a blessing.

These are just some of the great men of Ireland who studied and then trained others. They sought after God constantly, thus leaving behind the legacy that St Patrick had wished for. There were others, women too, whose stories may not be as well known or even recorded at all, for we know that thousands trained in Ireland's great monastic schools. Kuno Meyer, a late-nineteenth-/early-twentieth-century scholar, translated many Celtic poems and stories. He said that these Irish monks:

[through] carrying Christianity and a new humanism over Great Britain
and the Continent, became the teachers of whole nations, the counselors
of kings and emperors… the Celtic spirit dominated a large part of
the Western world, and Celtic ideals imparted a new life to a decadent
civilization…

CELTIC LEARNING AND ART

The ink of a scholar will survive longer than the blood of a martyr.
OLD IRISH SAYING

The Tradition

The druidic system that existed on the island before the arrival of Christianity already placed great value on learning. The druids trained for several years to achieve their status, and bards and poets were esteemed for their extensive expertise and wisdom. Knowledge was seen as power. Patrick and his followers provided Christian schools as an alternative to the druidic schools. The tradition held fast; while learning the Holy Scriptures was the primary focus in monasteries, the study of astrology, healing, and the old tales continued.

A country's knowledge is in its language, mythology, and mountains.

OLD IRISH SAYING

The first book of Scripture all monks learned – and, it logically follows, the first that all Irish Christians learned – was the book of Psalms. Memorizing the Psalter was their primary task, and every moment spent cooking, praying, walking, building, or engaging in any routine task involved the verses being spoken, often in song or chant. Other books of the Bible were memorized also. The Irish have always known that if you commit something to memory it is always with you.

When Patrick roamed Ireland the Irish essentially had no written language. The druids had a form of writing known as *ogham* used primarily to mark graves and boundaries, but not for recording stories. Once written language trickled down to the island in the late fifth century, the monastic centres took it up as a task given to them by God. Over the next couple of centuries they copied ancient texts, wrote down their own ancient tales, recorded monastic rules in verse and illustrated their books with colourful inks and imaginative drawings.

Even as early as the fifth century scholars travelled from Britain and Wales to study at the monastic schools in Ireland. Greek, a language that had essentially been forgotten in Europe at the time, was taught, thus preserving the ability to read and interpret the earliest Christian writings. Known for hospitality, the Irish welcomed students free of charge. In exchange, these pupils were expected to care for their masters in their old age. Learning was for all who would come. And they came in the thousands, prompting St Mailduff, an Irish founder of a monastery in Britain, to say, '[Ireland] literally blazed like the stars of the firmament with the glory of her scholars.' Columcille's love of learning and search for meaning was typical of many of the Irish. Through it, he hoped 'that I might search all books and from their chart find my soul's calm'.

Armagh, a great centre of learning, at one time housed 7,000 students. Other centres included those at Aran, Clonmacnoise, Glendalough, Cork, Innisfallen, Bangor and more. As the missionary monks travelled, other great schools sprung up in Europe, including Iona, most famous for the *Book of Kells;* Lindisfarne; and Bobbio, the Italian monastery founded by the great Irish saint Columban near the end of his life.

While European scholars valued the education available in Irish monasteries, the Irish came in droves to the European continent, where the word Irish came to be synonymous with scholar. So many Irish were employed by various lords and kings that one native scholar found cause to wonder whether any Irish were left in their own country. Not only did the monks migrate, but non-clergy did also, bringing their church with them. This was a great spiritual migration, as large parts of Europe had been overrun by pagan tribes and had thus lost much of its Christian heritage.

Some Scriptures were preserved in Ireland, while others were brought to the European continent for safekeeping during the Viking invasions. One such repository is St Gall's in St Gallen, Switzerland, founded by one of St Columcille's followers in 613. Gallus was an Irishman who, when Columcille was compelled to leave Italy, stayed in Switzerland to found his establishment. Some of the manuscripts residing at St Gall's date to the eighth century. Scholars who are interested in this era travel to conduct research in St Gall's library.

The ancient monk-scribes were not merely labourers, although they did work hard, savouring the bright sun for their work and continuing by candlelight except when producing the more delicate illuminated manuscripts. They were also learned men, well versed in Scripture and the old tales. However, transcription work was an important element of the Irish monastic life. While many ceremonial and treasured manuscripts were created, copied texts were often kept for personal use. Frequently there were little poems and sayings scribbled in the margins. Thankfully, the scribes were often lighthearted about their work and penned some revealing little verses, shedding light on what their days were like. Some of what they transcribed is still preserved for us today:

A hedge of trees surrounds me,
A blackbird's lay sings to me;
Above my lined booklet
The trilling birds chant to me.
In a grey mantle from the top of bushes
The cuckoo sings:
Verily – may the Lord shield me! –
Well do I write under the greenwood.

One popular poem is from either the eighth or ninth century, thought to have been penned by a student at St Paul's monastery in Carinthia, Austria. The story goes that it was composed on the back of a copy of St Paul's epistles (which of course was written in Latin). This clever poem was written in Irish. The unknown scribe was both witty and a little impish to do such a thing, but happily for us his creation gives a glimpse into his life. 'Pangur' is an old Irish name for cat and 'bán' means white.

I and Pangur Bán, my cat
'Tis a like task we are at;
Hunting mice is his delight
Hunting words I sit all night.

Better far than praise of men
'Tis to sit with book and pen;
Pangur bears me no ill will,
He too plies his simple skill.

'Tis a merry thing to see
At our tasks how glad are we,
When at home we sit and find
Entertainment to our mind.

68

Oftentimes a mouse will stray
In the hero Pangur's way:
Oftentimes my keen thought set
Takes a meaning in its net.

'Gainst the wall he sets his eye
Full and fierce and sharp and sly;
'Gainst the wall of knowledge I
All my little wisdom try.

When a mouse darts from its den,
O how glad is Pangur then!
O what gladness do I prove
When I solve the doubts I love!

So in peace our tasks we ply,
Pangur Bán, my cat, and I;
In our arts we find our bliss,
I have mine and he has his.

Practice every day has made
Pangur perfect in his trade;
I get wisdom day and night
Turning darkness into light.

TRANSLATED BY ROBIN FLOWER

The Books

Of all the works these monks produced, none is more famous than the *Book of Kells*, an illuminated manuscript written in approximately 800. The four Gospels, based on the Vulgate, are included along with the fourth-century prefaces, summaries and concordances originally composed by Eusebius of Caesarea. The

... intricacies, so delicate and so subtle, so full of knots and links, with colours so fresh and vivid, that you might say that all this was the work of an angel, and not of a man.

GERALD OF WALES, IN HIS *TOPOGRAPHIA HIBERNICA*, POSSIBLY SPEAKING OF THE *BOOK OF KELLS*

book is held today by Trinity College in Dublin and half a million people view a portion of the ancient book every year (there are 680 pages in total!).

The book was first mentioned in the eleventh century in the *Annals of Ulster* and was called *The Book of Columba*. Though there is some debate over where the book was written, most scholars concede that it was created at both the monastery in Iona and the one at Kells. No one knows for certain. There is some indication that the book is the work of several scribes and artists. It is believed to have gone missing from Iona during the Viking raids and later resurfaced at Kells, one of Columcille's foundations. The *Annals of Ulster* tells us that the book was stolen in 1006. It was soon recovered but without its jewelled cover – the only part raiders at the time were concerned with.

Around that time Gerald the Wise appears to have seen it, although at Kildare. No one knows how much this book may have travelled, but it seems to have had a home at Kells until the 1600s, when Archbishop James Ussher, or perhaps the successor of his seat in Meath, Henry Jones, presented it to Trinity College; it has resided there ever since. It's interesting to note that the book was never completed. There are outlines of drawings left unpainted.

The *Book of Kells* best typifies what people think of as an ancient Irish manuscript with its red, purple, black and yellow inks, its spiralling ornamentation and its animal designs. Nearly every page is decorated and some are purely illustrations. Actually, the book is unique rather than typical. The illustrations themselves show influences from various regions in the world, indicating that the monks either travelled or interacted with traders. While many ancient texts were illuminated most were not as art-filled, and some contained only text.

A certain amount of typical Irish humour does show up on its pages, however. One illustration shows a mouse running off with a communion wafer, and another shows a mouse hiding from a cat. The cat is scratching his head and biting his paw, wondering where the mouse has gone. Standing

right behind the cat, the mouse bears an identical expression that clearly shows that he does not know how to get out of his predicament. There are also cleverly concealed words in the illustrations. But beyond being witty, this book is truly a magnificent work of art and a national treasure – a labour of love for God.

Two more books cherished for their antiquity are the *Book of Durrow* and the *Antiphonary of Bangor*. The *Book of Durrow* may be the earliest illuminated manuscript to survive, dating to around 675. Like the *Book of Kells*, it is a book of the Gospels with portraits and lushly illustrated pages. Some scholars even suggest that the *Book of Durrow* was referred to in the making of the *Book of Kells*. The *Book of Durrow* also resides at Trinity College in Dublin. It is believed to have been created at Durrow Abbey, another of Columcille's monasteries, but some prefer Iona or Northumbria (Great Britain) as the place of origin. A farmer is said to have plunged the book into a cattle trough of water in an attempt to cure his herd of sickness, and there are indeed water stains on the pages. In light of such beliefs, it's a miracle that these books have survived for well over a millennium.

The *Antiphonary of Bangor*, composed sometime between 680 and 691, is the oldest surviving Irish prayer book. It consists of the prayers and chants spoken in the monasteries. Carried from Bangor to Bobbio, Columban's monastery, it is now housed in Milan. Many more ancient books have survived, most dating to a few centuries later.

The process of creating these books is almost as incredible as the works themselves. It began with preparing the necessary materials. The monks wrote on vellum or parchment, animal skins that had been soaked in lime and scraped clean of fat and hair. With that smelly task completed, the vellum sheets were stretched on a wooden frame and dried. For the *Book of Kells* calfskin was used, preferred for its white color. It is estimated that around 180 calves were needed to make the book.

Ink was carbon-based and made from natural dyes. Sometimes mineral extracts were used, and some of the resources came from faraway lands. The monks had to gather bark, flowers and other materials, pound them with wooden hammers until they had liquid (bark had to be removed from wood), add water, boil the liquid, add more water, and repeat as necessary. This is a simplification of the process; it was very time-consuming. Quill pens also had to be fashioned from goose or swan feathers, but before the eighth century pens were made from wood or metal. The pens or quills had to be sharpened continually, so the scribe kept a knife in reach. If the process of preparing the materials was not done well, the scribe's work was even more difficult. Some ancient manuscripts even contain complaints about the vellum or ink scribbled in the margins. The toil was considered worthwhile, even if laborious.

The fine illuminated manuscripts were the work of many scribes. One would be in charge of the layout, some would do the calligraphy (the text), others would work on the drawings, and still others would do the illumination or the colouring. These manuscripts were created during daylight hours – either candlelight was not strong enough to do the intricate work required or they feared the possibility of fire.

Everyday learning was aided by scratching on wooden tablets or any soft material with a wooden or metal stylus, and often these tablets were covered in wax for temporary note taking. Columcille is said to have learned his alphabet by writing it on a cake that he ate afterwards.

The Irish monks are credited with the invention of pocketbooks, small books that were carried in leather satchels. One such book from the ninth century miraculously survived in a bog in County Tipperary, from which it was unearthed in 2006. The conditions in Irish bogs have preserved many ancient treasures and even some human bodies. With several monastic ruins nearby, the theory that the Tipperary pocketbook was dropped there or hidden by a monk seems reasonable.

The survival of so many ancient Irish manuscripts is a remarkable blessing. One such book, the *Domhnach Airgid*, was for some time believed to have been written by St Patrick himself. Today, however, it is thought to date from around the eighth century, and its shrine, much later. Only recently have technological advances allowed the study of this book of the four Gospels, which is in fragments.

The High Crosses

Another outstanding feature of the ancient monasteries and churches is the stone high crosses, many of which are still standing. There may have been many purposes for the crosses, but some of them obviously were utilized as teaching aides. The average person in ancient Ireland could not read, and most did not have access to books if they could. Bible stories were told in pictures on many of these crosses. They are lavishly sculpted with biblical scenes from both the Old and New Testaments. St Martin's cross at Iona is an example and may be the oldest still standing, perhaps even original to Columcille's monastery.

Clonmacnoise's high cross, known as the Cross of the Scriptures, is another wonderful example. It is also referred to as King Flann's Cross because of an inscription stating that Colman erected it for King Flann. Some believe it marked the burial of this king. Dating from the ninth century, the cross is in excellent condition. Biblical scenes are carved on all sides of this 13-foot (4-metre) cross, which has been moved into an interpretation centre along with two others. Replicas now stand where the originals were.

The monastic site of Monasterboice near Drogheda in County Meath is the home of two more superb examples of Celtic high crosses. Muirdach's Cross is named for the abbot whose name appears on the base. Dating from the tenth century, the cross stands 16 feet (5 metres) high and depicts scenes such as the fall of Adam and Eve and Moses striking water from a rock. The crucifix is depicted in the centre of the cross on one side. Monasterboice's other cross, named the West Cross, is one of the tallest at approximately 21 feet (6.4 metres) and is the same vintage as Muirdach's Cross. Although more worn than Muirdach's Cross, its biblical scenes are still observable, such as Daniel hunting and Jesus with a crown of thorns.

Another magnificent high cross can be found at the ruins of Moone in County Kildare. This 17-foot (5.2-metre) tall cross is engraved on all sides with biblical depictions, including the twelve disciples, identical stout figures stacked in rows like toy soldiers. Making sure there were twelve would have been the most important objective for storytelling, and one can only imagine how difficult it must have been to carve those images from a huge slab of granite.

Other Relics

The ancient Irish Christians did not live in the grey stone world that the relics seem to suggest. They loved colour, and these crosses were most likely painted in the fashion of the *Book of Kells* and highly ornamented. The cells and churches and other buildings may have been decorated also. At the time Cogitosus wrote his account of Brigid he described the church at Kildare (rebuilt on the original site) as being decorated with paintings. He characterized a wooden partition as having painted images, and he noted the draped tapestries and a 'finely decorated' door. These descriptions leave a lot to the imagination, but certainly this church was not drab.

Some artefacts do survive from the early Irish churches, and processional crosses, ceremonial chalices and shrines – if not the buildings themselves – were highly ornate and embellished with jewels and glass and enamel ornaments. The finest example is the Ardagh Chalice, which resides at the National Museum in Ireland and dates from the ninth century. These were the kinds of treasures that later attracted Norse raiders. The natural world beamed with colour: emerald green grass; blue skies; the black, white and orange puffin; white sea birds; purple heather – all these things were painted by God, the Master Artist. The Celts would have chosen similar colours in what they created.

Celtic Learning and Art

Non-Monastic Learning

Learning in ancient Ireland was achieved in many ways. Everyone was schooled in one manner or another, whether formally in Greek and Latin or in the occupational trades such as metalworking, farming or needlework.

Many who did not go to the monastic schools went to what were called bardic schools, where they learned stories and tales orally and practised repeating them. Nearly every family group had someone who entertained with these stories. There were degrees of achievement in nearly every field, just as there are in secondary schools today. The top level of bard had to know more than 300 tales by heart. Someone at this level was heard at court before kings and travelled from place to place throughout the countryside. Noblemen sometimes hired these bards to reinvent history and depict them in a more favourable light. Traditional Irish storytelling continued even after these tales were written down in books. Those who carried on the tradition, and still do, are called *seanchaithe* (singular: *seanchaí*).

Because information spoken in verse is much more easily remembered, the Irish bards told their stories in song. Some played a harp or were accompanied by musicians. The tradition of music in Ireland has a very long history. This old Irish saying shows the value that the Celts placed on stories and songs: 'There are two versions of every story and at least twelve versions of every song.'

The Spiritual Blessing of Celtic Learning

An old Irish adage says, 'If we are without knowledge of our past, then we are without knowledge of ourselves.' While the ancient Irish took seriously the study of their ancestors and the paths they travelled, we have a challenge today if we want to do the same. Unlike them we are not likely to labour just to write a sentence. Books are no longer treasures, because they are easily obtained and information can be gleaned in many other ways as well. The supernatural character of the old tales causes the modern mind to quickly dismiss them.

Human dependence on the earth that nurtures us often goes unnoticed. And yet, because these early Irish men and women once preserved knowledge and shared it, there is hope that the same thing can be accomplished today. The vast access to knowledge that we now have would have been wholeheartedly embraced by the ancients. If we study with the same zeal our forebears had, if we recite the stories to our children and others, if we refuse to let obstacles deter us from valuing the Celtic wisdom and knowledge handed down to us, then the path they trod will be unveiled for us, and for others as well.

But the model of Celtic learning should not be viewed as a scientific equation for spiritual growth. The Celts learned with their hearts, following the model of Jesus' disciple John who told his stories in a deeply emotional, heartfelt manner. His spirituality came from within. Along with his brother James, he was nicknamed 'Son of Thunder', and the Celts related to his passion. It was John who quoted Jesus this way: 'I am come that they might have life, and that they might have it more abundantly' (John 10:10). Life for them was full: full of joy and sometimes grief, but always rich with creative fervour.

The Irish Christians' preference for the apostle John ran counter to Rome's inclination for the apostle Peter. Truly both were disciples of Jesus and are equally worthy of study, but an examination of how the Celts learned and loved, and how John's spiritual side influenced them, can begin to bring our own souls into harmony with what the Creator God intended.

To find the spiritual blessing of learning that the Celts experienced, do what they did. Value wisdom. Look at life not only with the eyes, but also with the heart. Wonder at the miracles existent in nature. Use rhyme, song, rhythm – whatever it takes to remember the truths you have been taught. Seek solitude. Be disciplined. Give generously. Teach others. Blessings occur when one realizes that God is already present.

CELTIC PRAYER

O you who hear prayer,
to you all men will come.

PSALM 65:2

The Celtic Difference

The reason Christianity developed differently in Ireland than it did elsewhere is because the faith had a monastic base. And the reason monasticism took root is because ancient Ireland consisted of a system of tribes, groups of family members ruled by a king. The concept of an abbot (who was quite frequently a member of the region's royal family) who shepherded faithful followers was quite natural for the Irish. The Roman organization of a bishop overseeing religious matters in a city that was ruled by another man, a king (none of them necessarily related to each other), was unnatural to the Irish.

Because the Christian movement was monastic, the practice of prayer was different also. Prayer was not reserved primarily for church; it was a natural outpouring of the culture, a culture that saw power in the natural world, one that did not see a division between the spiritual and the secular, one that did not judge worthiness – Jesus died for all. The Irish prayers reflected the life of the people and were melodic, continual and close to the heart.

Even the early Irish monastic rules differed, both from each other and from the orderly Western rules of St Benedict, the founder of Western monasticism in the sixth century. St Benedict's rules were straightforward and to the point. The Irish rules were sometimes written in verse, and while still clear and pointed, they were in some cases more philosophical and poetic, such as the rule of St Ailbe, a supposed disciple of St Patrick: 'the good of your soul should take precedence over the good of your body'. From the rule traditionally assigned to the abbot Cormac Mac Ciolionáin: 'the melodious chant of the believers is as food to me'.

Christ Within and Without

Just as the concept of *peregrinatio* (pilgrimage) had no ultimate earthly goal, so it often was with prayer. An inner longing, placed within by God, prompted one to pray in praise and thanksgiving and to invite the Holy Spirit to accompany the person praying and keep him or her safe.

The following poem serves to remind us that while God is everywhere, seeking him without first encountering him within is futile:

> *To go to Rome*
> *Is much of trouble, little of profit:*
> *The King whom thou seekest here,*
> *Unless thou bring Him with thee, thou wilt not find.*

TRANSLATED BY KUNO MEYER

A lesser-known figure from early Irish Christian history is Samthann of Clonbroney. She once told someone who wished to devote his life to prayer and travel abroad, like many were doing at that time, that if God were not to be found in Ireland, then everyone should go overseas. However, the path to God can be found in all lands.

Just as in 'St Patrick's Breastplate', the acknowledgment and desire for God to be ever before the mind of the believer is passed down through the centuries. The following prayer is from a book dating from the sixteenth century:

God be in my head
and in my understanding;
God be in my eyes
and in my looking;
God be in my mouth
and in my speaking;
God be in my heart
and in my thinking;
God be at my end
and at my departing.

The ancient belief was that the spiritual realm was not far from humans even while they were still earthly bound. In fact, nearly every ancient Irish Christian poem and hymn in some way reflects this. The essence of Celtic Christianity – according to many theologians – is this awareness that earth and heaven, angels and saints, are as near to us as our earthly brothers and sisters. Again, this belief was handed down from the pagan ancestors, and it was as natural to the ancient Irish Christians as a rainy morning, though it may be hard for us to understand today. Family for them went beyond the immediate core and those they met day to day and even beyond the present, to generations of old. Everyone is a co-inheritor of what God provides on earth. That is why the spiritual was, and in

The Lord is my strength and my song; he has become my salvation.

PSALM 118:14

some cases still is, contained in the everyday speech of the Irish. '*Dia dhuit*' ('God with you') is the traditional greeting, and '*Dia is Muire dhuit*' ('God and Mary with you') is the appropriate response.

Christ Before, Christ Behind

While there are many prayers in the Bible, the ancient Irish Christians chose to memorize the Psalms (which were offered as prayers) more than any other book. The Irish monks memorized all the Psalms, but Psalm 118 was most often recited due to its spirit of thankfulness and its call upon God for protection. With each repetition (one physical step for each verse) one came ever closer to God.

The Celts also prayed what were called Circling Prayers. These prayers were appeals for protection and called for some things to be within the circle and some to be outside it. For example:

> Circle me, Lord.
> Keep peace within, keep harm without.
> Circle me, Lord.
> Keep love within, keep hate without.

Whatever one wished to pray about could be inserted into this prayer, whether it was an illness (health within and sickness without), a journey (fair weather within, storms without) or any other concern. Parts of 'St Patrick's Breastplate' offer an example of things to keep without: 'Against all Satan's spells and wiles, against false words of heresy, against the knowledge that defiles, against the heart's idolatry', and so on.

Spiritually Interwoven

In the ancient Celtic mind the line between many things the modern mind perceives either did not exist or was fluid: heaven and earth, day and night,

In his hand is the life of every creature
and the breath of all mankind.

JOB 12:10

and the seasons, for example. All things were connected; all creation flowed
in harmony and to an ancient rhythm that many today have forgotten. The
Celtic knot is a visual portrayal of something that is so interwoven that the
beginning cannot be discerned, nor the ending. This is also seen in Celtic prayer,
which blends together praise, thankfulness, adoration and petitions into one.
The spiritual is the physical and the physical is the spiritual. Like so many of
the ancient stories that contain both fact and myth, the spiritual realms could
neither be separated nor distinguished in the Celtic mind. Therefore, not just the
Creator's handprint but the Creator himself can be found in all of life.

Praise Every Day

Praise was essential in the old Celtic prayers, and that is why the book of
Psalms, with its verses of thanksgiving and reverence for the natural world,
was a natural fit. An example comes from the last chapter in Psalms:

Praise the Lord.
Praise God in his sanctuary;
praise him in his mighty heavens.
Praise him for his acts of power;
praise him for his surpassing greatness.
Praise him with the sounding of the trumpet,
praise him with the harp and lyre

PSALM 150:1–3

For a people whose livelihoods depended largely on factors they could
not control – the weather, invasions, illness – prayers of thankfulness
came freely and frequently. In pagan times, different gods were believed to
control those various factors, and they had to be appeased; sacrifices were
offered. With the new faith, sacrifices were no longer needed, because of
Jesus' sacrifice for all, so this tradition was naturally turned into prayers

Celtic Prayer

of praise: for the sunrise, for good crops, for health, and, conversely, breastplate-type prayers were said against bad things.

There is a line in 'St Patrick's Breastplate' that says, 'In every place and in all hours'. Likewise, when Samthann was asked whether the correct position for praying was lying down, sitting or standing, she replied that a person should pray in every position. That is the Celtic thought on prayer. While liturgy certainly had its place for these ancient people, a personal, continuous conversation with God was both who they were on the outside and what they were made of on the inside.

Blessings were sought before any journey was undertaken, whether across the sea like Brendan the Navigator's adventure or just to the cow barn. The midwife said prayers over a newborn child, even if a priest was to bless the infant later. There was no instance when prayers or blessings were not spoken by the ancient Irish Christians. Praying was so ingrained that they couldn't help but pray. The presence of God was always assumed.

Finding God in Nature

Prayer is the attempt to connect and communicate with the spiritual. With the physical and spiritual intermingled, like the fretwork and intricate designs the Celts were so fond of, nature was revered as it had been with the pagan ancestors. The Irish monk Pelagius said, 'There is no creature on earth in whom God is absent.' The Christians saw nature as the handiwork of God and evidence of his presence, not as individual gods. This belief was reflected in their prayers, prayers that were spoken outside of church and not confined to silence. Generations learned these prayers because they were spoken aloud and often. An example of a much-repeated prayer follows:

Deep peace, pure gold of the sun to you.
Deep peace, pure white of the moon to you.
Deep peace, pure blue of the sky to you.
Deep peace, pure green of the grass to you.

Deep peace, pure brown of the earth to you.
Deep peace, pure grey of the dew to you.
Deep peace, of the running wave to you.
Deep peace, of the whispering trees to you.
Deep peace, of the flowing air to you.
Deep peace, of the quiet earth to you.
Deep peace, of the shining stars to you.
Deep peace, of the Son of Peace to you.

Erin (Éire), the Irish word for the island of Ireland, was the mother of life to the ancient Irish. The earth provided everything needed for sustenance: fruit in the trees, grass for the cattle, water for drinking, soil for planting. But the importance of the land is something all too soon forgotten in the modern world. Erin is the indication of the hand of God. Again, the Psalms were confirmation of a belief the ancient Irish already held: 'The heavens declare the glory of God; the skies proclaim the work of his hands' (Psalm 19:1).

Columban expressed this when he said, 'Understand the creation, if you wish to know the Creator.' Likewise the ninth-century Irish philosopher John Scotus Eriugena believed that if God's voice were silent, creation would cease to exist. Since we have so many writings from Columcille available to us, we are able to observe this close tie to nature in the form of Celtic prayers:

Delightful would it be to me
From a rock pinnacle to trace
Continually
The Ocean's face:
That I might watch the heaving waves
Of noble force
To God the Father chant their staves
Of the earth's course.

That I might mark its level strand,
To me no lone distress,
That I might hark the sea-bird's wondrous band –
Sweet source of happiness.
That I might hear the clamorous billows thunder
On the rude beach.
That by my blessed church side I might ponder
Their mighty speech.
Or watch surf-flying gulls the dark shoal follow
With joyous scream,
Or mighty ocean monsters spout and wallow,
Wonder supreme!
That I might well observe of ebb and flood
All cycles therein.

ATTRIBUTED TO ST COLUMBA, FROM *THE CELTIC PSALTERY* BY ALFRED PERCEVAL GRAVES

There were also poems, which for the Irish were prayers, to celebrate the seasons, pointing yet again to the Irish love and appreciation of nature:

Summer has come, healthy and free,
Whence the brown wood is bent to the ground:
The slender nimble deer leap,
And the path of seals is smooth.

FROM 'SUMMER HAS COME', TRANSLATED BY KUNO MEYER

Deep-red the bracken, its shape all gone –
The wild-goose has raised his wonted cry.
Cold has caught the wings of birds;
Season of ice – these are my tidings.

FROM 'SUMMER IS GONE', TRANSLATED BY KUNO MEYER

Evening, and morning, and at noon, will I pray,
and cry aloud: and he shall hear my voice.

PSALM 55:17

Sometimes this reverence for nature is mistaken for nature worship. Celtic Christians believe that God is in all things, not that all things are gods. The distinction is important, and it became a point of transformation once the pagan Irish followed the God of Patrick. To take delight in nature, as is evident in these poems, is to pray to and adore the God who is responsible for creating it.

Prayer was integrated into the natural rhythm of life. There were designated times of prayer, especially for monks. The days were divided into seven Offices (services of prayers and psalms), likely based on the following verse from the book of Psalms: 'Seven times a day do I praise thee because of thy righteous judgments' (Psalm 119:164). The Offices occurred in the middle of the night, dawn, the beginning of the workday, noon, mid-afternoon, sunset and compline, which was the completion of the day. At the conclusion of compline many communities practised silence until dawn. These hours of prayer were usually announced by the tolling of a bell. Mirroring life's rhythm – day into night, season following season – prayer followed a course.

Whether the ancient Irish were monks or clergy or just ordinary people, they followed some kind of pattern in their prayers, including those before bed, such as, 'May Thou holy angels, O Christ, son of living God, guard our sleep, our rest, our shining bed' and 'I lay me down with God; May He rest here also. His Guardian arms around my head. Christ's Cross my limbs below' (from *The Celtic Psaltery* by Alfred Perceval Graves).

Prayers of Longing

All souls, not only the Celtic soul, are restless. The Irish monks became wanderers precisely because of this longing to find their hearts' desire. Originally an eighth-century Irish prayer, the hymn 'Be Thou My Vision' beautifully expresses the Celtic soul's longing for God:

Be thou my vision, O Lord of my heart
Naught be all else to me, save that thou art;
Thou my best thought in the day and the night,
Waking or sleeping, thy presence my light.

Be thou my wisdom, be thou my true word,
I ever with thee, and thou with me, Lord;
Thou my redeemer, my love thou hast won;
Thou in me dwelling, and I with thee one.

Riches I heed not, nor vain empty praise,
Thou mine inheritance through all my days;
Thou, and thou only the first in my heart,
High King of heaven, my treasure thou art!

High King of heaven, thou heaven's bright sun,
Grant me its joys after vict'ry is won;
Christ of my own heart, whatever befall,
Still be my vision, O Ruler of all.

TRANSLATED BY MARY E. BYRNE, VERSED BY ELEANOR H. HULL (1912)

We are all on a journey that takes us through this life and on toward the next. The ancient Irish had a phrase for this: *Slí na fírinne*, or the path to truth. It was often used in reference to people who had died, and it still is, but it can also be applied to this journey which has no ending here on earth. With the belief that life was a journey, an ever-changing adventure that they couldn't possibly foresee or completely understand, it's no wonder they were eager and ready to wander about the vast ocean in a rudderless boat. St Columban expressed the belief that in order for God to answer prayer, one has to search God out. He said, 'He must yet be besought by us, often besought; ever must we cling to God, to the deep, vast, hidden, lofty, and almighty God.'

Celtic Prayer

The following prayer illustrates the searching, the longing to find the path to God:

> *Jesu, from to-day*
> *Guide us on our way,*
> *So shall we, no moment wasting,*
> *Follow Thee with holy hasting,*
> *Led by Thy dear Hand*
> *To the Blessed land.*

FROM *THE CELTIC PSALTERY* BY ALFRED PERCEVAL GRAVES

Prayer That God Hears

Prayer was not a selfish pursuit in ancient Ireland. Christians saw Christ in others because, like the hills and the seas and the animals of the earth, humans are creations of God. Because of this all-embracing view they were able to keep the faith as an outreach rather than as an inward journey of self-study. An old Irish saying illustrates this: 'Prayer should be cast wide.'

Prayers of confession were important to the ancient Christians who used the Bible and their ancient concept of *anamcara* (soul friend) to guide them. Praying for someone else was just as important as having someone hear your confession and pray for you. The belief was that interceding in prayer for others prompted God to open his ears and grant a blessing. A desire for God to hear one's prayers was just as important to the ancient Irish Christians as it was to the psalmist when he said, 'I call on you, O God, for you will answer me; give ear to me and hear my prayer' (Psalm 17:6).

Prayer was not seen only as a personal uplifting of spirit. Prayers of adoration were offered to the God who desired to be close to his creation, who indeed dwelled in all creation. A ninth-century Irish hymn of praise was inspired by Revelation 7:12. In that passage we are told that angels surrounding the throne of God are continually praising him, and such constant praise to the king was the desire of the Celtic Christian also. The hymn took up this scripture and added to it:

Knowledge and gratefulness
Reverence and esteem
Majesty and power
To the eternal God.

Singing and praises
Heartfelt blessings
Measureless outpouring
To the Trinity of Heaven.

Ceaseless adoration
Boundless thanksgiving
Infinite might
To God forever and ever.

AUTHOR'S INTERPRETATION OF AN ANCIENT PRAYER

In the same way that the ancient Irish assumed the presence of God, they believed their prayers were heard because they felt God near them. A wonderful example of the belief that God is not far away is found in Maelisu's 'Hymn to the Holy Spirit'. This hymn, or prayer, also echoes 'St Patrick's Breastplate' as a call for protection:

O Holy Spirit, hasten to us!
Move round about us, in us, through us!
All our deadened souls' desires
Inflame anew with heavenly fires!

Yea! let each heart become a hostel
Of Thy bright Presence Pentecostal,
Whose power from pestilence and slaughter
Shall shield us still by land and water.

From bosom sins, seducing devils,
From Hell with all its hundred evils,
For Jesus' only sake and merit,
Preserve us, Thou Almighty Spirit!

FROM *THE CELTIC PSALTERY* BY ALFRED PERCEVAL GRAVES

The Spiritual Blessing of Celtic Prayer

One of the most difficult things to grasp is seeing the eternal God within others and ourselves. The truth today is that God is still here, but we are often blind to him. The Celtic monk Pelagius said that God is visible, because everywhere 'narrow shafts of divine light pierce the Veil that separates heaven from earth'. Praying for the ability to see with fresh eyes is a simple but profound prayer. Again, Pelagius said, 'The presence of God's spirit in all living things is what makes them beautiful; and if we look with God's eyes, nothing on the earth is ugly.' At the turn of the twentieth century Celtic scholar Douglas Hyde, who would later become the first President of Ireland, published a book of Irish poems and prayers that he acquired from people, letters, and manuscripts all over Ireland in the hope of preserving some of the tradition that was beginning to fade away. The sample below illustrates the Celtic yearning to acknowledge God and to grow in his love:

My God, my life, my love, my light,
My strength, my joy, my treasure,

Celtic Prayer

Let it be my thought both day and night
In Thee to take my pleasure.
Increase my love, my sighs, my groans
My careless lips to move it,
And let my thoughts be fixed alone
On Jesus, Mary and Joseph.

The ancient path is illuminated for anyone who would fix their thoughts and learn from those who have travelled it. By hearing their stories, attuning to their words of wisdom, and trusting that he who led them will lead others today, the listener, the seeker, the wayfarer can travel that same course and find God all along the way. As the Irish say, 'Let ancient things prevail.' Look for the ancient path. Ask. Listen. Take up that road and find rest for your soul.

Bibliography

Bladey, Conrad, *Brigid of the Gael, A Guide for the Study of St. Brigid of Kildare, A Sourcebook for Classroom Use* (Linthicum, MD: Hutman Productions, 2000)

Cahill, Thomas, *How the Irish Saved Civilization, The Untold Story of Ireland's Heroic Role from the Fall of Rome to the Rise of Medieval Europe* (NY: Doubleday, 1995)

Chadwick, Nora, *The Age of Saints in the Early Celtic Church* (London: Oxford University Press, 1963; first published in 1961)

Dames, Michael, *Mythic Ireland* (London: Thames and Hudson, 1992)

Davies, Oliver, ed., *Celtic Spirituality*, (NY: Paulist Press, 1999)

De Waal, Esther, *The Celtic Way of Prayer, The Recovery of the Religious Imagination* (NY: Image Books, Doubleday, 1997)

De Waal, Esther, *Every Earthly Blessing, Rediscovering the Celtic Tradition* (Harrisburg, PA: Moorehouse Publishing, 1991)

Dillion, Myles and Nora Chadwick, *The Celtic Realms, The History and the Culture of the Celtic Peoples From Pre-History to the Norman Invasion* (Castle Books, 2003)

Hunter, George G. III, *The Celtic Way of Evangelism, How Christianity Can Reach the West... Again* (Nashville: Abingdon Press, 2000)

Joyce, P. W., *A Smaller Social History of Ancient Ireland* (London: Longmans, Green, and Co., 1908; 2nd edition)

Knowles, Joseph A., *St Brigid, Patroness of Ireland* (Brown and Nolan, 1907)

LeHane, Brendan, *The Quest of Three Abbots, The Golden Age of Celtic Christianity* (Hudson, NY: Lindisfarne Press, 1994; first published in 1968)

MacManus, Seumas, *The History of the Irish Race* (CT: Konecky & Konecky, 1921)

McCaffrey, Carmel and Leo Eaton, *In Search of Ancient Ireland, The Origins of the Irish from Neolithic Times to the Coming of the English* (Chicago: Ivan R. Dee, 2002)

Moorhouse, Geoffrey, *Sun Dancing, Life in a Medieval Irish Monastery and How Celtic Spirituality Influenced the World* (San Diego: Harcourt Brace & Company, 1997)

Newell, J. Philip, *Listening For the Heartbeat of God, A Celtic Spirituality* (NJ: Paulist Press, 1997)

Ó Duinn, Seán OSB, *The Rites of Brigid, Goddess and Saint* (Dublin: The Columba Press, 2005)

O'Hanlon, John, *Lives of the Irish Saints: With special festivals, and the commemorations of holy persons, complied from calendars, martyrologies, and various sources, relating to the ancient church history of Ireland*, Vol. 5 (Dublin: James Duffy and Sons, 1875; 1st edition)

Ó Maidín, Uinseann, trans., *The Celtic Monk, Rules & Writings of Early Irish Monks* (Kalamazoo, MI: Cistercian Publications, 1996)

Staunton, Michael, *The Voice of the Irish, The Story of Christian Ireland* (NJ: Hidden Spring, Paulist Press, 2001, 2003)

Slavin, Michael, *The Ancient Books of Ireland* (Montreal: McGill-Queen's University Press, 2005)

Picture Acknowledgments

pp. 2–3: Mountains near a lake, Lough Derryclare, Connemara, County Galway, IIC/Axiom/Getty Images

pp. 4–5: Dinish Island, Kenmare Bay, County Kerry, IIC/Axiom/Getty Images

p. 6: Steps in the wild garden, Glanleam House, County Kerry, IIC/Axiom/Getty Images

p. 9: Morning mood in the Wicklow Mountains, blickwinkel/Alamy

p. 12: Conor Pass on the Dingle Peninsula, The Irish Image Collection/Corbis

pp. 14–15: Stone circles, Inchquinn, County Kerry, IIC/Axiom/Getty Images

p. 19: Teamhair Na Riogh (Hill of Tara) in County Meath, The Irish Image Collection/Photolibrary

p. 24: Ahalia River near Maam Cross in Connemara, County Galway, imagebroker/Alamy

p. 27: St Brigid's Cathedral, County Kildare, The Irish Image Collection/Corbis

p. 32: Abandoned farmhouse in the Irish Countryside, Richard Cummins/Corbis

p. 36: Rainbow over Ballyferriter Bay on the Dingle Peninsula, County Kerry, nagelestock.com/Alamy

pp. 40–41: Dunluce Castle overlooking the sea, County Antrim, David Noton/Getty Images

p. 44: A patchwork of emerald fields from Croaghaun Hill with the Comeragh Mountains in the background, County Waterford, George Munday/Alamy

p. 49: The Mac Regol Gospels, ninth-century Irish manuscript written and illuminated by Mac Regol (d. 822), Abbot of Birr, County Offaly (Bodleian shelf mark Auct D 2 19 folio 1r), The Art Archive/Bodleian Library Oxford

p. 54: The view towards Mount Brandon and Owenmore Valley at dawn, Conor Pass, Dingle Peninsula, County Kerry, Frank van der Zwan/Alamy

p. 61: Glendalough, County Wicklow, scenicireland.com/Christopher Hill Photographic/Alamy

p. 64: Dunguaire Castle, Kinvera, County Galway, Tom Mackie/Alamy

p. 70: St Matthew from the *Book of Kells*, c. 800, The Print Collector/Photolibrary

p. 75: Celtic Cross, Dingle, Morgan Hei /Alamy

p. 78: Waterfall, Sloughin Glen, County Tyrone, The Irish Image Collection/Photolibrary

p. 83: Moss growing on trees, Killarney National Park, Halaska Jacob/Index Stock Imagery/Photolibrary

p. 88: Sunset on Clare Island, County Mayo, Travelpix Ltd/Getty Images

p. 93: Irish road, William Huber/Getty Images